for
GIRLS
Only!
DEVOTIONS

for GIRLS Only!
DEVOTIONS

CAROLYN LARSEN

illustrated by
LEAH SUTHERLAND

Tyndale House Publishers, Inc. Carol Stream, Illinois

Visit Tyndale's exciting Web site for kids at www.tyndale.com/kids.

TYNDALE and Tyndale's quill logo are registered trademarks of Tyndale House Publishers, Inc.

For Girls Only! Devotions

Designed by Jessie McGrath

Edited by Stephanie Voiland

Unless otherwise indicated, all Scripture quotations are taken from the *Holy Bible*, New Living Translation, copyright © 1996, 2004, 2007 by Tyndale House Foundation. Used by permission of Tyndale House Publishers, Inc., Carol Stream, Illinois 60188. All rights reserved.

Scripture quotations marked NIV are taken from the *Holy Bible*, New International Version®. NIV®. Copyright © 1973, 1978, 1984 by International Bible Society. Used by permission of Zondervan. All rights reserved.

For manufacturing information regarding this product, please call 1-800-323-9400.

Library of Congress Cataloging-in-Publication Data

Larsen, Carolyn, date.
  For girls only! devotions / Carolyn Larsen ; illustrated by Leah Sutherland.
    p. cm.
  ISBN 978-1-4143-2209-4 (sc)
  1. Girls—Religious life—Juvenile literature. I. Sutherland, Leah. II. Title.
  BV4551.3.L37 2009
  242'.62—dc22   2009019559

Printed in the United States of America

15 14 13 12 11 10

7 6 5

For Cori and Mallory . . . my girls. You continue to teach me so much about living and loving.

Contents

Sticks and Stones

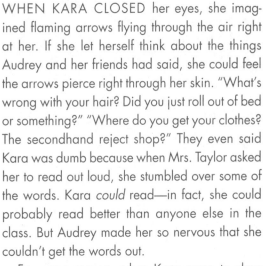

The tongue is a small thing that makes grand speeches. But a tiny spark can set a great forest on fire.

JAMES 3:5

WHEN KARA CLOSED her eyes, she imagined flaming arrows flying through the air right at her. If she let herself think about the things Audrey and her friends had said, she could feel the arrows pierce right through her skin. "What's wrong with your hair? Did you just roll out of bed or something?" "Where do you get your clothes? The secondhand reject shop?" They even said Kara was dumb because when Mrs. Taylor asked her to read out loud, she stumbled over some of the words. Kara *could* read—in fact, she could probably read better than anyone else in the class. But Audrey made her so nervous that she couldn't get the words out.

For some reason, when Kara came to class midway through the year, Audrey decided she didn't like her. Kara was so shocked by Audrey's mean comments that tears rolled down her face before she could stop them. That was all Audrey needed to keep up the abuse. When she found out she could get away with bullying Kara, she did so every chance she got.

Some people only feel good about themselves when they are cutting others down. Maybe they don't know how much their words hurt other people. Maybe they even think they are being funny. It's no fun to be on the receiving end of sarcastic comments. The negative things settle into your heart and make it difficult to feel good about yourself.

Most people don't realize how much their words affect others. But God knows that the things we say have the power to help or hurt people. We are encouraged in the Bible to speak kindly to each other. We are told to be careful how we speak to each other—to guard our tongues. Jesus taught that we should show love to others. A big part of showing love means being careful about what we say and thinking about how our words will make the other person feel.

CHECKUP TIME

On a scale of 1 to 5, how thoughtful are you in how you speak to others?

1 = never
2 = not very often
3 = sometimes
4 = most of the time
5 = always

I think about how my words will make others feel—before I say them.
1   2   3   4   5

I try to say things in a kind way, even when it's a difficult thing to talk about.
1   2   3   4   5

I make an effort to show God's love to others in all I do and say.
1   2   3   4   5

I ask God to help me always speak in love.
1   2   3   4   5

I try to be kind to everyone, not just my friends.
1   2   3   4   5

KEY

MOSTLY 1s Uh-oh, you'd better stop and think about how you feel when someone speaks unkindly to you.

MOSTLY 2s You've taken some baby steps toward kindness. Keep moving in the right direction.

MOSTLY 3s Average is the best we can say. Not bad, but could be better.

MOSTLY 4s You're showing some Christlike attitudes and actions. Great job.

MOSTLY 5s Excellent! You share God's love by how you speak to and treat others.

THINGS TO DO

☐ Think of someone your group of friends has treated badly in the past. Talk with your friends about one genuinely nice thing you can do for that person.

☐ List some good qualities of a person you're tempted to speak unkindly to.

☐ Say at least one kind thing every day . . . to a different person each day.

☐ Memorize a Bible verse about speaking kindly, such as Psalm 39:1 or Colossians 3:17. Post it on your mirror or in your locker, and say it to yourself several times a day.

THINGS TO REMEMBER

Let us think of ways to motivate one another to acts of love and good works.
HEBREWS 10:24

If you are kind only to your friends, how are you different from anyone else? Even pagans do that. **MATTHEW 5:47**

I will watch what I do and not sin in what I say.
PSALM 39:1

The lips of the godly speak helpful words, but the mouth of the wicked speaks perverse words.
PROVERBS 10:32

Whatever you do or say, do it as a representative of the Lord Jesus, giving thanks through him to God the Father. **COLOSSIANS 3:17**

If someone were to pay you ten cents for every kind word you ever spoke and collect five cents for every unkind word, would you be rich or poor?
UNKNOWN

As perfume to the flower, so is kindness to speech.
KATHERINE FRANCKE

No act of kindness, no matter how small, is ever wasted.
AESOP

Family Night

May the Lord make your love for one another and for all people grow and overflow.

1 THESSALONIANS 3:12

HALEY WOULD DENY it if any of her friends asked, but seriously, she thought Friday night was the best night of the week! She looked forward to it—not just because the weekend meant no school. She loved Friday night because it was family night. Phone calls went to voice mail, the computer was turned off, no friends came over, and everyone stayed home.

Family night was just for the family. They had pizza or hot dogs for dinner. Then they played games or watched a movie together. It was always something different. But the truth was, it didn't really matter what they did. The best part was just that they were all together: Mom, Dad, Haley, her sister, and her brother. No matter how the night began, they usually ended up laughing really hard. Dad talked in his silly cartoon voice, and sometimes Mom laughed so hard she cried. It was actually pretty fun.

Did you know that families were God's idea? He knew that it would be good for you to have a family to love you and support you—no matter what! Some families are made up of a mom and a dad and their children. Some families are just one parent and the kids, or a parent and a stepparent and the kids. Some families are related genetically, and some are connected by adoption. Some families even include grandmas and grandpas or aunts and uncles and cousins.

Sometimes you may get frustrated with the

rules at your house or with the chores you have to do. Or maybe you have a little brother who is a total pain or an older sister who is sometimes bossy. But the bottom line is that God gave you your family—whatever your family is like—to love and encourage you through good times and bad . . . and so you can do the same for each of them!

CHECKUP TIME

I treat my brothers and sisters with respect and love.

1   2   3   4   5

I obey the rules that have been set up at my house and do my chores without complaining.

1   2   3   4   5

I speak respectfully to my parents and grandparents.

1   2   3   4   5

I encourage my family members when they try new things.

1   2   3   4   5

I pray for my family each day.

1   2   3   4   5

KEY

MOSTLY 1s Whoa, you'd better read this devotion again and think seriously about how much your family means to you.

MOSTLY 2s At least you know you *have* a family, but you've got some work to do.

MOSTLY 3s Just average. You can do better.

MOSTLY 4s Not bad. You appreciate being a part of a family.

MOSTLY 5s Excellent! You love and respect your family. Keep it up!

THINGS TO DO

- ☐ Do one chore this week without being asked, to show your parents how much you appreciate them.
- ☐ Suggest a family night for your family and plan out the first one.
- ☐ Think of two nice things to say about each person in your family—then say them!
- ☐ Thank God for your family and all they do for you.

THINGS TO REMEMBER

God himself has taught you to love one another. **1 THESSALONIANS 4:9**

My child, listen when your father corrects you. Don't neglect your mother's instruction. **PROVERBS 1:8**

A wise child accepts a parent's discipline; a mocker refuses to listen to correction. **PROVERBS 13:1**

Honor your father and mother, as the LORD your God commanded you. **DEUTERONOMY 5:16**

Children, obey your parents because you belong to the Lord, for this is the right thing to do. **EPHESIANS 6:1**

Look for the good, not the evil, in the conduct of members of the family.
JEWISH PROVERB

You don't choose your family. They are God's gift to you, as you are to them.
DESMOND TUTU

A brother is a friend provided by nature.
LEGOUVE PERE

Living with an Attitude

"WHY DO I have to clean my room?" Emma whined to her mom. "My friends are going to the pool. I'm the only one who has to do chores. It's not fair."

Lately it seemed that Emma had a bad attitude about almost everything. She didn't want to do her homework. She complained that her clothes weren't as new as her friends' clothes and that she had too many rules. She didn't want to do her share of chores around the house. Emma's bad attitude affected everyone else too. Her brothers and sisters were beginning to act in the same negative, whiny way. Even Mom and Dad found themselves fighting a bad attitude when Emma was around.

The weird thing was that Emma didn't even realize how much her negative attitude was dragging her down until she and Mom talked about it. After that she made a real effort to not complain so much. She was a lot more pleasant to be around . . . and she found she was a lot happier herself when her attitude was better!

Did you know that if one apple in a basket begins to spoil, the rottenness will spread to all the apples around it? The same is true of a bad attitude. If one person is constantly whining and complaining and being negative about everything, pretty soon others will be negative too. Bad attitudes spread quickly. So either your bad attitude brings others down too or they begin avoiding you. After all, who wants to be around someone who is always complaining?

Where does a bad attitude come from? It starts in your heart, often from your being self-centered and wanting things your own way. Then it spreads to your thoughts and quickly takes over your mind. Before you know it, your attitude is coming out of your mouth. Several times in the Bible we are told to guard our hearts—maybe because that's where the attitude battle starts in the first place.

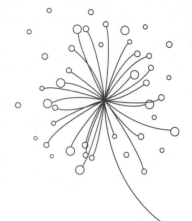

CHECKUP TIME

On a scale of 1 to 5, how is your attitude?

1 = never
2 = not very often
3 = sometimes
4 = most of the time
5 = always

I know my attitude affects the attitudes of others.
1   2   3   4   5

When I feel a bad attitude coming on, I get busy improving it.
1   2   3   4   5

I accept it when I don't get my way.
1   2   3   4   5

I think about what I say and how it sounds to others.
1   2   3   4   5

I have a good attitude, even when I have to do something I'd rather not do.
1   2   3   4   5

KEY

MOSTLY 1s It sounds like you are the Queen of Whiners. Choose one of the statements from the quiz above and get to work on improving in that area.

MOSTLY 2s Well, you're not the worst, but you do have some work to do.

MOSTLY 3s Average. Not bad, but could be better.

MOSTLY 4s You realize that having a bad attitude is not pleasant. But you can still improve.

MOSTLY 5s Excellent! You show God's love with a good attitude!

THINGS TO DO

☐ Write a "thanks for all you do" note for someone in your family and leave it on the kitchen counter.

☐ Next time you hear yourself whining about getting your own way, stop yourself, then do an attitude check.

☐ Ask God to help you notice when your attitude is really bad. Then ask for his forgiveness and help in apologizing to any people you have hurt.

☐ When you're tempted to complain, stop and think of three things you can be thankful for.

THINGS TO REMEMBER

Fix your thoughts on what is true, and honorable, and right, and pure, and lovely, and admirable. Think about things that are excellent and worthy of praise. **PHILIPPIANS 4:8**

Think about the things of heaven, not the things of earth. **COLOSSIANS 3:2**

Don't look out only for your own interests, but take an interest in others, too. **PHILIPPIANS 2:4**

You must have the same attitude that Christ Jesus had. **PHILIPPIANS 2:5**

Let the Spirit renew your thoughts and attitudes. **EPHESIANS 4:23**

You are more likely to act yourself into feelings than feel yourself into action.
JEROME BRUNER

Nothing in life is so hard that you can't make it easier by the way you take it.
ELLEN GLASGOW

Reflect upon your present blessings, of which every man has plenty; not on your past misfortunes, of which all men have some.
CHARLES DICKENS

The Long, Long Night

MADDIE COULDN'T SLEEP. She tried counting sheep (wonder who ever thought of that idea?). Didn't work. She read for a while. That didn't work either. It was like her mind wouldn't shut off. And why were her thoughts racing? Maddie was *mad*! Really mad! Rachel, who was supposed to be her best friend in the whole world, said something really mean about Maddie. At least, that's what Lizzie told Jill, who told Maddie.

Maddie couldn't believe that Rachel would say that. At first she was really hurt, but then she just got plain old mad. When Rachel tried to talk to her after school, Maddie just brushed right past her without saying a word. Now Maddie was wide awake, getting madder every minute. In her mind, she was rehearsing every word of what she'd say to Rachel about how she felt. Maddie imagined that there was going to be a major fight . . . and she was definitely going to win!

Whoa! Maybe there was a better way Maddie could have handled this. After all, Rachel was her best friend in the whole world. Perhaps Maddie could have talked to her to find out if what Jill heard from Lizzie was even true. It would really stink if their friendship was ruined over something that wasn't even true. Plus, it would mean that Maddie was wide awake over nothing! God knows how worked up we can get. It's crazy how we can write these complicated scripts in our minds that build up little tiny mole-hills into big mountains in no time!

That's why God instructs us in the Bible to deal with anger right away. Don't let it roll around in your heart and mind all night. It will only cause more problems if you let it settle in. So as soon as possible, talk to the person who hurt you or made you angry. Sometimes your anger is caused by a misunderstanding. Sometimes you have a right to be angry, but you can still talk it through, settle it, forgive the person, and get on with life . . . and get a good night's sleep!

CHECKUP TIME

On a scale of 1 to 5, how well do you handle your anger?

1 = never
2 = not very often
3 = sometimes
4 = most of the time
5 = always

I get the facts from the person who has made me angry . . . right away.
1   2   3   4   5

I stop the fictional arguments in my mind, where I always win.
1   2   3   4   5

I check out the truth instead of believing rumors.
1   2   3   4   5

I ask God to help me control my temper.
1   2   3   4   5

When I'm angry, I speak kindly and listen to the other person's responses as I explain my feelings.
1   2   3   4   5

KEY

MOSTLY 1s Yikes! You are one angry girl. Choose one statement from the quiz above and start working on improving that.

MOSTLY 2s Well, you're not the worst, but you still have some anger to deal with.

MOSTLY 3s Not bad, but you could do better at letting things go.

MOSTLY 4s Pretty good, but there's a little room for improvement.

MOSTLY 5s Excellent! Anger doesn't control you, and God's love shines through.

THINGS TO DO

☐ Next time you hear a rumor, let it stop with you instead of passing it on to others.

☐ When your temper starts rising, stop, count to ten, and take a deep breath. Ask God to help you be kind.

☐ Write down three good qualities of each of your friends.

☐ When your friend does something that upsets you, give her a chance to explain before you get mad.

THINGS TO REMEMBER

Stop being angry! Turn from your rage! Do not lose your temper—it only leads to harm. **PSALM 37:8**

Understand this, my dear brothers and sisters: You must all be quick to listen, slow to speak, and slow to get angry. **JAMES 1:19**

If you are even angry with someone, you are subject to judgment! **MATTHEW 5:22**

A gentle answer deflects anger, but harsh words make tempers flare. **PROVERBS 15:1**

[Love] is not irritable, and it keeps no record of being wronged. **1 CORINTHIANS 13:5**

People who fly into a rage always make a bad landing.
WILL ROGERS

For every minute you are angry you lose sixty seconds of happiness.
RALPH WALDO EMERSON

If you kick a stone in anger, you'll hurt your own foot.
KOREAN PROVERB

Cheaters Never Win

The LORD detests the use of dishonest scales, but he delights in accurate weights.
PROVERBS 11:1

THE SPELLING BEE winner would get to ride in a stretch limo to a nearby fast-food restaurant for lunch, and there would be a story about her in the local newspaper. Then, of course, she would get to go on to the next level of competition. The school would throw a party for her. All the other students would cheer her on. So cool!

Sara wanted to win the bee more than anything else in the world. In fact, she wanted to win so badly that she planned out a way she could win for sure . . . even though it wasn't exactly fair. There were only a few words she really had trouble with. So Sara wrote them very lightly on the palms of her hands. Then, when she was given one of those words during the bee, she just sneaked a look at her hand and correctly spelled the word. It seemed like a great idea . . . until Mrs. Ramones noticed her looking at her hand. And just like that, Sara was disqualified. No limo ride. No newspaper story. No next level of competition. Lots of embarrassment. And worst of all, a guilty conscience because she cheated.

When you want something very much but you know it's going to take a lot of hard work to get it, you may be tempted to cheat. But it's never worth it. Even if Sara hadn't gotten caught— even if she'd won the spelling bee—in her heart she would have known that she won unfairly. There's not much to be proud of when you win like that. In fact, in God's eyes, that's not really winning at all.

The Bible is very clear on the topic of cheating. God is no fan of cheaters. Honesty is best, because honest people always win. Oh sure, they may not get first place in a spelling bee, but they know in their hearts that they acted with integrity and did their best. That's a victory in itself!

AARDVARK
VACUUM
GNAT

CHECKUP TIME

On a scale of 1 to 5, how well do you handle the temptation to cheat?

1 = never
2 = not very often
3 = sometimes
4 = most of the time
5 = always

I understand that doing things honestly is more important than winning.

1   2   3   4   5

I study hard so I'm not as likely to be tempted to cheat.

1   2   3   4   5

I get help when I need it rather than cheating.

1   2   3   4   5

I understand that God takes cheating seriously.

1   2   3   4   5

When my "need to win" attitude gets in the way, I confess it to God.

1   2   3   4   5

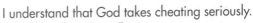
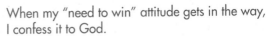

KEY

MOSTLY 1s Did you forget that cheaters never win? Choose one statement from the quiz above and get busy working on it.

MOSTLY 2s Honesty is not at the top of your list, is it?

MOSTLY 3s Average, average, average. Not bad, but needs to be better.

MOSTLY 4s You're doing pretty well, but there's a little room for improvement.

MOSTLY 5s Great! Honesty is a priority for you!

THINGS TO DO

☐ God will help you with the temptation to cheat. Memorize Luke 16:10 and repeat it to yourself when you are tempted.

☐ Write down three things you enjoy and are good at. Thank God for the ability to do those things.

☐ Using a notebook or calendar, come up with a study or practice plan, so you're prepared for your next test or competition and can do your best.

☐ Make a pact with your friends to be encouraging instead of competitive with each other.

THINGS TO REMEMBER

If you are faithful in little things, you will be faithful in large ones. But if you are dishonest in little things, you won't be honest with greater responsibilities.
LUKE 16:10

The LORD demands accurate scales and balances; he sets the standards for fairness.
PROVERBS 16:11

It is better to be godly and have little than to be evil and rich. **PSALM 37:16**

Cling to your faith in Christ, and keep your conscience clear. For some people have deliberately violated their consciences; as a result, their faith has been shipwrecked.
1 TIMOTHY 1:19

Do not deceive or cheat one another.
LEVITICUS 19:11

He who purposely cheats his friend, would cheat his God.
JOHANN KASPAR LAVATER

Honesty is the best policy.
MIGUEL DE CERVANTES

I would prefer even to fail with honor than to win by cheating.
SOPHOCLES

It's All about Me!

"GUESS WHAT? My mom is going to let me try out for the chorus!" Katie was so excited she could hardly breathe. She had run all the way to Ella's house to share her happy news. Ella had been in chorus for the past two years . . . but she wasn't so happy. Katie didn't even notice. "I know I can make it. It will be so cool! Chorus looks like so much fun! I've seen all the new friends you've made and the supercool costumes you wear, and I know about the trips you get to go on. I can't wait!"

Ella knew she should say something nice. But she couldn't make herself do it. The truth was, she didn't want Katie to join the chorus. Chorus was hers! She liked being in it, and she liked that most of her friends thought she was special because she was a chorus member. Ella liked when her friends came to hear the concerts. She liked when they oohed and aahed over the costumes. But she didn't like the idea of Katie being in the chorus. That would make it less special for her! Besides, Ella knew she was a much better singer than Katie. She doubted Katie could even pass the audition test.

There is a fine line between being proud to be a part of something (that's a good thing) and being filled with pride in yourself (that's a bad thing). It wouldn't hurt to do a little reflection: Is your mouth often filled with praises of yourself? Is your mind sometimes full of self-congratulations?

If so, you might need to rethink the way you see yourself and other people. It's impossible to encourage others or celebrate their successes if you always want to be number one. Living the way that Jesus lived doesn't leave any room for pride in yourself. Jesus didn't focus on himself; he served others and encouraged them to be better and better.

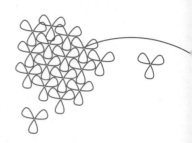

CHECKUP TIME

On a scale of 1 to 5, how are you doing at avoiding pride?

1 = never
2 = not very often
3 = sometimes
4 = most of the time
5 = always

I welcome others into my activities.
1   2   3   4   5

I think about how my attitude makes others feel.
1   2   3   4   5

I am humble about my abilities and talents.
1   2   3   4   5

I understand that life isn't all about me.
1   2   3   4   5

I am happy for my friends when they are successful.
1   2   3   4   5

KEY

MOSTLY 1s Wow, did you ever wonder if your proud attitude is keeping you from having friends? Ask God to help you with this whole pride issue.

MOSTLY 2s Humbleness is not at the top of your list, is it?

MOSTLY 3s Average, average, average. Not bad, but needs to be better.

MOSTLY 4s You're doing pretty well, but you can still work on your prideful attitude.

MOSTLY 5s You understand the difference between healthy pride and bad pride.

THINGS TO DO

☐ Make a list of the things you're good at and see if you have healthy pride or the bad kind of pride about them.

☐ Compliment one person every day about something they have done well.

☐ Write someone a note of congratulations when he or she has accomplished a difficult task.

☐ Thank God for the gifts and talents he has given you.

THINGS TO REMEMBER

If you try to hang on to your life, you will lose it. But if you give up your life for my sake, you will save it. **MATTHEW 16:25**

Stop acting so proud and haughty! Don't speak with such arrogance! For the LORD is a God who knows what you have done; he will judge your actions. **1 SAMUEL 2:3**

You rescue the humble, but your eyes watch the proud and humiliate them. **2 SAMUEL 22:28**

God opposes the proud but favors the humble. **JAMES 4:6**

Love is patient and kind. Love is not jealous or boastful or proud. **1 CORINTHIANS 13:4**

I long to accomplish a great and noble task, but it is my chief duty to accomplish humble tasks as if they were great and noble. The world is moved along, not only by the mighty shoves of its heroes, but also by the aggregate of the tiny pushes of each honest worker.
HELEN KELLER

Pride makes us artificial and humility makes us real.
THOMAS MERTON

A proud man is always looking down on things and people; and, of course, as long as you're looking down, you can't see something that's above you.
C. S. LEWIS

Whatever . . .

AMANDA'S FRIENDS HAD their own ideas of what was fun. Some of their choices were not so good—like sneaking through a neighborhood at night and checking to see if any cars were unlocked. When they found one, they took something from inside as a trophy of their success. Or sometimes they hung around the mall and dared each other to steal things—nothing big, but then again, it was still stealing.

Of course, Amanda knew these things were wrong. After all, she had grown up going to church and reading her Bible. She had asked Jesus into her life. . . but what her friends were doing was just no big deal to her. She didn't want to make them mad at her or have them think she was weird or something. So she just went along with them and laughed when they laughed and ran when they ran. No big deal.

No big deal? Really? Amanda was making a definite choice here. She was choosing to disobey what she knew was the right way to live. Stealing is never okay. Breaking God's commandments is never okay. Amanda might have thought she could just say, "Whatever . . ." and go along with her friends without taking any responsibility for what was happening. Not so. She was brushing off her responsibility to live in a way that honors Christ. Her faith was lukewarm, and that's not good!

God wants people who follow him completely,

not halfheartedly. People with a lukewarm faith tend to show up at church or youth group and say all the right things. Maybe they even pray impressive-sounding prayers, but when they are back with their friends, they do whatever they want, regardless of what they may have just learned at church or youth group. What some people don't realize is that when it comes to taking a stand for what is right, not to decide is to decide. Okay, read that again: *not* to decide *is* to decide. Either we obey what we know to be right or we don't. There is no middle of the road.

CHECKUP TIME

On a scale of 1 to 5, where do you stand on the issue of obedience?

1 = never
2 = not very often
3 = sometimes
4 = most of the time
5 = always

I act the same with my church friends as I do with my other friends.
1   2   3   4   5

I take my faith and my Christian life seriously.
1   2   3   4   5

I have a close group of people to hang out with who encourage me in my Christian walk.
1   2   3   4   5

I stand up for what's right, even if it means going against the crowd.
1   2   3   4   5

I am honest about the sins in my life and understand that all sin matters.
1   2   3   4   5

KEY

MOSTLY 1s Wow! If you looked up *lukewarm* in the dictionary, your picture would be there!

MOSTLY 2s Do your school friends even know you're a Christian?

MOSTLY 3s Average, average, average. Not bad, but you can do better.

MOSTLY 4s There's room for improvement, but you're doing pretty well.

MOSTLY 5s Excellent! You take your relationship with God seriously.

THINGS TO DO

☐ Next time you're faced with a tough decision, choose to follow what you know to be right, regardless of what your friends do.

☐ If you see your friends about to make a bad decision, encourage them to do what's right.

☐ Make a list of the people you spend most of your time with, then evaluate how they are influencing you. If necessary, choose different friends to hang out with.

☐ Ask a friend to keep you accountable about acting in a way that pleases God, whether you're around other Christians or not.

THINGS TO REMEMBER

I know all the things you do, that you are neither hot nor cold. I wish that you were one or the other! But since you are like lukewarm water, neither hot nor cold, I will spit you out of my mouth!
REVELATION 3:15-16

You adulterers! Don't you realize that friendship with the world makes you an enemy of God? I say it again: If you want to be a friend of the world, you make yourself an enemy of God. **JAMES 4:4**

Choose today whom you will serve. . . . As for me and my family, we will serve the LORD.
JOSHUA 24:15

If you love me, obey my commandments.
JOHN 14:15

If someone claims, "I know God," but doesn't obey God's commandments, that person is a liar and is not living in the truth. **1 JOHN 2:4**

Whatever you do, don't do it halfway.
BOB BEAMON

The ultimate measure of a man is not where he stands in moments of comfort and convenience, but where he stands at a time of challenge and controversy.
MARTIN LUTHER KING JR.

To choose what is difficult all one's days, as if it were easy, that is faith.
W. H. AUDEN

I Hate You!

Your love for one another will prove to the world that you are my disciples.
JOHN 13:35

"NO, YOU CANNOT hang out at the mall all evening. You're not old enough to do that." Mom's answer was quiet but firm.

"Mom, come on. All my friends are going. It's no big deal," Rebecca whined.

"Rebecca, I said no. Case closed."

"Why do you have to be so mean? I hate you!" Rebecca screamed. She ran into her bedroom and slammed the door as hard as she could, threw herself onto the bed, and hid her face in a pillow. Disappointment and anger boiled inside her. "She treats me like a baby. I wish I could just run away. I hate her!" Rebecca felt like her mom was being unfair—she had too many rules, and she was much stricter than all her friends' moms.

Have you ever felt that angry at your parents or at another person? Despite what she said, Rebecca doesn't actually hate her mother. The word *hate* represents a very strong emotion. It's thrown around a lot, like when people say, "I hate broccoli" or "I hate that kind of music" or even "I hate you." We often use the word when we don't really mean it. However, it's a good idea to stop and think about what we're saying before we open our mouths.

Jesus taught that we should love one another. He said that the first and most important commandment is to love God with all your heart, soul, mind, and strength and that the second commandment is just as important—to love your neighbor as yourself. Love is what it's all about: love God and love other people. So when someone makes you really angry, stop and think about your response before shouting, "I hate you!" If Rebecca had done that, she might have realized that she didn't really hate her mom; she was just disappointed that she couldn't go to the mall.

Remember that the most important (and most difficult) time to show love is when you're responding out of a strong negative emotion—when you're disappointed or unhappy with what someone has said or done. Don't spout hate words. Take a deep breath and respond in love.

CHECKUP TIME

On a scale of 1 to 5, how are you doing in the love department?

1 = never
2 = not very often
3 = sometimes
4 = most of the time
5 = always

I think before spouting out what comes into my mind.
1   2   3   4   5

I respond with patience instead of anger when I feel like something is unfair.
1   2   3   4   5

I understand that my parents' rules are meant to help me become more mature and responsible.
1   2   3   4   5

I try to react and respond with love.
1   2   3   4   5

I apologize when I haven't treated someone with love.
1   2   3   4   5

KEY

MOSTLY 1s Wow, you have some major work to do. Make an effort to begin today!

MOSTLY 2s Not the bottom of the list, but you can certainly improve.

MOSTLY 3s Average, average, average. Not bad, but needs to be better.

MOSTLY 4s There's room for improvement, but you're doing pretty well.

MOSTLY 5s Great job! You show love in your words and actions.

THINGS TO DO

- ☐ Try to stop using the word *hate* . . . for good.
- ☐ When you're angry, count to ten before saying a word.
- ☐ Respectfully ask your parents to explain any rules you don't understand.
- ☐ Ask God to help you speak and act with love.

THINGS TO REMEMBER

There is no greater love than to lay down one's life for one's friends. **JOHN 15:13**

Love covers a multitude of sins.
1 PETER 4:8

No one has ever seen God. But if we love each other, God lives in us, and his love is brought to full expression in us. **1 JOHN 4:12**

Hatred stirs up quarrels, but love makes up for all offenses. **PROVERBS 10:12**

We should love one another. This is not a new commandment, but one we have had from the beginning. **2 JOHN 1:5**

Know this: though love is weak and hate is strong, yet hate is short, and love is very long.
KENNETH BOULDING

We can do no great things; only small things with great love.
MOTHER TERESA

One word frees us of all the weight and pain in life. That word is love.
SOPHOCLES

Standing on the Sidelines

SADIE STOOD NEAR the wall of the cafeteria and watched a group of her classmates laughing and talking. They seemed to be having a lot of fun, and she longed to join them. It was hard to come to lunch day after day and eat alone, especially when she could hear the other girls having so much fun. Sadie wanted a friend—just one friend to tell her secrets to and laugh and talk with. A couple of weeks ago, she got brave enough to sit at the lunch table where one group of girls usually sat. When they came in, they politely asked her to move down a little, and then they sat down and turned their backs to her while they laughed and talked. Sadie finally got up and left without eating her lunch. She didn't understand why she couldn't find a friend. Sadie was so lonely.

No one was intentionally being mean to Sadie. They just didn't seem to notice her, and she wasn't doing much to change things. Just sitting at a table where other girls sat but not saying anything to them wasn't going to get their attention. To be a friend, you must be friendly. There are many ways to make a friend, but sometimes you have to take an extra step and be the first one to start the conversation. One thing to remember is that you need to stop focusing on yourself and how you feel. Think about others and what they may be feeling. The Bible says to do to others what you would like them to do for you. So treat others the way you would like to be treated.

Is it scary to take the first step to talk to someone? Yeah, it is! But it's one way to show you're interested in becoming someone's friend. Try it—it just might work!

CHECKUP TIME

On a scale of 1 to 5, how friendly are you?

1 = never
2 = not very often
3 = sometimes
4 = most of the time
5 = always

I show I'm interested in others and what's going on in their lives.
1   2   3   4   5

I make an effort to talk to people who seem lonely.
1   2   3   4   5

I understand that people I don't know may be just as scared to talk to me as I am to talk to them.
1   2   3   4   5

I include other people in conversations and activities, even if they aren't part of my usual group of friends.
1   2   3   4   5

I ask forgiveness when I've excluded someone.
1   2   3   4   5

KEY

MOSTLY 1s Wow, you have some major work to do. Choose one specific thing to work on this week.

MOSTLY 2s If you want to have friends, you've got to work on being a friend.

MOSTLY 3s Middle of the road—try to become more aware of others.

MOSTLY 4s There's room for improvement, but you're doing pretty well.

MOSTLY 5s You are a friend, and you have friends!

THINGS TO DO

- ☐ Ask someone you trust to tell you whether or not you appear approachable.

- ☐ Start up a conversation today with one person you don't know very well.

- ☐ Look around for people on the edge of the crowd and talk to one of them.

- ☐ Be intentional about smiling more than you frown.

THINGS TO REMEMBER

Be kind to each other, tenderhearted, forgiving one another, just as God through Christ has forgiven you.
EPHESIANS 4:32

A friend is always loyal, and a brother is born to help in time of need. **PROVERBS 17:17**

Since God chose you to be the holy people he loves, you must clothe yourselves with tenderhearted mercy, kindness, humility, gentleness, and patience.
COLOSSIANS 3:12

The most important commandment is this: "Listen, O Israel! The LORD our God is the one and only LORD. And you must love the LORD your God with all your heart, all your soul, all your mind, and all your strength." The second is equally important: "Love your neighbor as yourself." No other commandment is greater than these. **MARK 12:29-31**

Let's not merely say that we love each other; let us show the truth by our actions. **1 JOHN 3:18**

The shortest distance between two people is a smile.
VICTOR BORGE

A true friend is someone who thinks that you are a good egg even though he knows that you are slightly cracked.
BERNARD MELTZER

My best friend is the one who brings out the best in me.
HENRY FORD

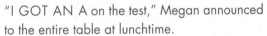

Not a Word of Truth

"I GOT AN A on the test," Megan announced to the entire table at lunchtime.

"You didn't get an A," Emily shot back. "That test was really hard."

"I did too. In fact, I've got an A in math for the whole term." Megan sort of lifted her head and looked arrogantly at the other girls. She seemed to be daring someone to argue with her. No one did.

But no one believed her. Megan had developed a reputation. Plain and simple, everyone knew that Megan lied. She lied about her grades, how much money her family had, the exciting things they did on vacation . . . pretty much everything. She always seemed to be trying to impress people with how smart or important she was. Too bad it didn't work. Her friends didn't trust a thing she said. Even when she told the truth, no one believed her.

Sometimes lying about something seems like such a good idea at the time. You might think, *One little lie is no big deal. No one will know.* But the thing is, if you tell one little lie, then you have to tell another one to cover up the first one, and then another to smooth over the last one, and on and on. Once you start lying about things, it becomes a habit, and the need to impress people or protect yourself becomes so tempting that lying appears to be the only answer.

Besides the fact that there is no future in lying, God has very plainly stated his opinion about lying: it's wrong! The Bible makes it clear that God is a God of truth, and lying does not please him. That means lying is a sin, and you can't lie your way out of that!

CHECKUP TIME

On a scale of 1 to 5, how honest are you?

1 = never
2 = not very often
3 = sometimes
4 = most of the time
5 = always

I make sure what I'm going to say is the truth before I open my mouth.
1   2   3   4   5

I believe that telling the truth is pleasing to God.
1   2   3   4   5

I think honesty is the best policy, even if it means I get in trouble.
1   2   3   4   5

I encourage my friends and family to tell the truth.
1   2   3   4   5

I forgive people who have lied to me.
1   2   3   4   5

KEY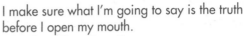

MOSTLY 1s If you were Pinocchio, your nose would be a mile long!

MOSTLY 2s You've got some honesty work to do.

MOSTLY 3s So-so. You can do better.

MOSTLY 4s There's room for improvement, but you're doing pretty well.

MOSTLY 5s Congratulations! You are an honest, trustworthy person.

THINGS TO DO

☐ Apologize to one person you've lied to and tell him or her the truth.

☐ Say a prayer for someone who has lied to you. Ask God for the ability to forgive that person.

☐ Thank your friends for liking you for who you are.

☐ Ask a friend to be your accountability partner. Help each other stick with telling the truth and nothing but the truth.

THINGS TO REMEMBER

The LORD detests lying lips, but he delights in those who tell the truth. **PROVERBS 12:22**

There are six things the LORD hates—no, seven things he detests: haughty eyes, a lying tongue, hands that kill the innocent, a heart that plots evil, feet that race to do wrong, a false witness who pours out lies, a person who sows discord in a family. **PROVERBS 6:16-19**

Stop telling lies. Let us tell our neighbors the truth, for we are all parts of the same body.
EPHESIANS 4:25

We will speak the truth in love, growing in every way more and more like Christ. **EPHESIANS 4:15**

Keep your tongue from speaking evil and your lips from telling lies! **PSALM 34:13**

Sin has many tools, but a lie is the handle which fits them all.
OLIVER WENDELL HOLMES SR.

Oh what a tangled web we weave when first we practice to deceive!
SIR WALTER SCOTT

The simple step of a courageous individual is not to take part in the lie. One word of truth outweighs the world.
ALEXANDER SOLZHENITSYN

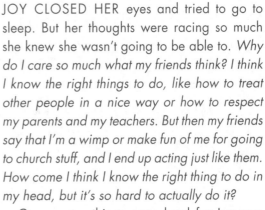

I Don't Know What to Do

Jesus replied, "All who love me will do what I say."
JOHN 14:23

JOY CLOSED HER eyes and tried to go to sleep. But her thoughts were racing so much she knew she wasn't going to be able to. *Why do I care so much what my friends think? I think I know the right things to do, like how to treat other people in a nice way or how to respect my parents and my teachers. But then my friends say that I'm a wimp or make fun of me for going to church stuff, and I end up acting just like them. How come I think I know the right thing to do in my head, but it's so hard to actually do it?*

One reason things were hard for Joy was because she was so focused on what other people thought of her. She didn't want them to think she was weird or something. She felt like she got teased enough as it was, and she wanted to fit in.

Joy was in a tough place because she was trying to ride the fence between living a Christian life and doing what her friends did. This can be a confusing place to be, because we all struggle with wanting to be liked and wanting to do the right thing. But trying to follow God and obey him only when it is convenient—like when your friends aren't around—just does not work. Trying to be a part-time Christian will keep your heart and mind bouncing around like a tennis ball as you decide first one thing is right, then something else. There's no doubt confusion will have control of you.

There is a simple answer to this, although it certainly is not always the *easy* thing. The simple answer is to obey and honor God—all the time, no matter who is around to see. The Bible says that God brings clarity, not confusion, to his children. So when you read his Word, pray, and listen to him, he will clear up the things that have you mixed up. When Joy tries that, she will know the right things to do and say. Bye-bye, confusion!

CHECKUP TIME

On a scale of 1 to 5, how is your Christian walk?

1 = never
2 = not very often
3 = sometimes
4 = most of the time
5 = always

I choose to do what is right—even if my friends are doing something different.
1   2   3   4   5

I read God's Word to find direction and guidance.
1   2   3   4   5

When I'm confused, I ask God for help.
1   2   3   4   5

I choose friends who also want to honor and obey God.
1   2   3   4   5

I am willing to lovingly confront my friends when they are making bad choices.
1   2   3   4   5

KEY

MOSTLY 1s This will never do. Choose one thing to focus on and get moving in the right direction.

MOSTLY 2s There is definitely room for improvement.

MOSTLY 3s Okay, you're starting in the middle, so get moving!

MOSTLY 4s Yeah, it's tough, but you're doing pretty well.

MOSTLY 5s Good job. Your walk with God is consistent!

THINGS TO DO

☐ When you're confused about what to do, ask someone you trust for advice.

☐ Make a list of things a follower of Christ should and should not do. It's easier to stick to your beliefs if you nail them down before the pressure comes.

☐ If your friends are doing something you know isn't right, choose to go home instead of joining them.

☐ Ask God for strength to help you obey.

THINGS TO REMEMBER

Be careful to obey all these commands I am giving you. Show love to the LORD your God by walking in his ways and holding tightly to him.
DEUTERONOMY 11:22

Praise the LORD! How joyful are those who fear the LORD and delight in obeying his commands.
PSALM 112:1

When you obey my commandments, you remain in my love, just as I obey my Father's commandments and remain in his love. **JOHN 15:10**

Don't just listen to God's word. You must do what it says. Otherwise, you are only fooling yourselves. For if you listen to the word and don't obey, it is like glancing at your face in a mirror. You see yourself, walk away, and forget what you look like.
JAMES 1:22-24

Joyful are those who obey his laws and search for him with all their hearts. **PSALM 119:2**

Character is doing the right thing when nobody's looking.
J. C. WATTS

One act of obedience is better than one hundred sermons.
DIETRICH BONHOEFFER

Nothing shall be lost that is done for God or in obedience to Him.
JOHN OWEN

Secret Sins

Day and night your hand of discipline was heavy on me. My strength evaporated like water in the summer heat.

PSALM 32:4

JULIE DID ALL she could to prepare for the math test. She did all her homework. She did practice problems all week. Julie wanted to do well on the test. She really did. But math was so hard for her. Julie had not been good at math since the beginning, when she learned addition and subtraction in first grade. Every year it got more confusing. The thing Julie was good at was spelling. She could figure out how to spell just about any word by sounding it out. Julie's friend James was really good at math but not so good at spelling.

So the two of them came up with a plan. Their desks were conveniently next to each other in both language arts and math. So the day of the math test, James kind of slid his paper over to the right so Julie could peek over and see his answers. In language arts class, Julie did the same for him. They knew it was cheating, but they were sure no one would ever know. It was their little secret, and they both got pretty good grades in spelling and math.

Well, here's the deal: maybe Julie and James would get away with their little scheme. Maybe the teachers would never know and they would both get better grades in their classes. But would that mean they really got away with anything? Nope. Even if their teachers or classmates never found out, there is still one person who would know about their secret sin. Who? God.

It is impossible to keep secrets from God. He knows all the thoughts and ideas in your heart. He knows your activities—all of them—even the ones you try to hide. And in God's eyes, things that are wrong are always wrong, even if they are done in secret. Sin is still sin, plain and simple, even if you don't get caught. Fooling God is not possible, so don't even try. Live honestly before him—in secret and out in the open.

CHECKUP TIME

On a scale of 1 to 5, how open are you before God?

1 = never
2 = not very often
3 = sometimes
4 = most of the time
5 = always

I evaluate my heart and my thoughts to see if they're pleasing to God.
1   2   3   4   5

I understand that I can't fool God. He sees everything.
1   2   3   4   5

I ask God to forgive me when I've tried to hide something from him.
1   2   3   4   5

I believe that honesty is more important than success.
1   2   3   4   5

I ask God to help me fight the temptation to cheat.
1   2   3   4   5

KEY

MOSTLY 1s Really? You think your secret sins escape God's notice? Confess your secrets to him right now, and start working on improving.

MOSTLY 2s There is definitely room for improvement.

MOSTLY 3s Right in the middle. You can do better!

MOSTLY 4s Pretty good. Keep going.

MOSTLY 5s Good job. Your relationship with God is open and honest!

THINGS TO DO

☐ Honestly examine your secret thoughts and see if they are honoring to God.

☐ With God's help, try to change one secret habit that dishonors him.

☐ Every morning, think through the day ahead and times you might be tempted toward a secret sin. Pray in advance for God's help in avoiding those temptations.

☐ Memorize a verse about God's strength helping you, such as Psalm 18:32 or Ephesians 3:16.

THINGS TO REMEMBER

For the honor of your name, O LORD, forgive my many, many sins.
PSALM 25:11

God arms me with strength, and he makes my way perfect. **PSALM 18:32**

I pray that from his glorious, unlimited resources he will empower you with inner strength through his Spirit. **EPHESIANS 3:16**

Dear friends, you always followed my instructions when I was with you. And now that I am away, it is even more important. Work hard to show the results of your salvation, obeying God with deep reverence and fear. **PHILIPPIANS 2:12**

We can be sure that we know him if we obey his commandments. **1 JOHN 2:3**

We are free to sin, but not to control sin's consequences.
J. KENNETH KIMBERLIN

The knowledge of sin is the beginning of salvation.
LATIN PROVERB

Sin is too stupid to see beyond itself.
ALFRED LORD TENNYSON

Just Downright Mean!

Do to others as you would like them to do to you.
LUKE 6:31

BROTHERS CAN BE such a pain in the neck. Saige knew that for sure. Her brother was four years older, and he made her life miserable. For some reason, Jason thought it was hilarious to sneak into her room and pull pranks on her. Yeah, really funny. He put oatmeal in her bed, squeezed all her toothpaste into the sink, and hid half her shoes . . . the left ones. Worse than all that, Jason threatened to make up lies about her and tell their parents unless she agreed to do half of his chores and keep quiet about all his tricks. Of course, if Saige tried to get back at Jason in any way, he went right to their parents and complained.

Some people (not just brothers) think it's okay to treat other people any way they want. They make a habit of giving others a hard time, being rude or just downright mean. But then they think that those same people they have been mistreating should always be kind and helpful to them. The Bible has something to say about the way we should interact with each other. In fact, it's expressed in one simple verse: treat other people the way you want to be treated (see Luke 6:31).

Makes sense, doesn't it? Be kind to others, and there is a good chance they will be kind right back. Be mean to others, and there is a good chance they will be mean back to you. That doesn't mean Saige's problems will disappear if she treats her brother right. (In fact, she should probably talk to her parents about what's going on.) But even though she can't control his actions toward her, she can control the way she responds. The key to living in a godly way is to think about others and how your words and actions make them feel. You can't really do that if you're always thinking about yourself and if you consider your feelings more important than anyone else's. God says it's important to show love to others, even if they don't show you love first. Treating others the way you would like to be treated is a good way to begin showing them love.

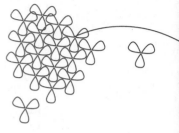

CHECKUP TIME

On a scale of 1 to 5, how do you treat others?

1 = never
2 = not very often
3 = sometimes
4 = most of the time
5 = always

My goal is to show God's love to others.
1   2   3   4   5

I care about other people and how I make them feel.
1   2   3   4   5

When I'm hurt, I ask God to guide my words and actions.
1   2   3   4   5

When I'm tempted to be unkind, I stop and think before I open my mouth.
1   2   3   4   5

I treat others the way I'd like to be treated.
1   2   3   4   5

KEY

MOSTLY 1s Wow! In your mind, the world is all about *you*, isn't it?

MOSTLY 2s There is definitely room for improvement.

MOSTLY 3s Right in the middle. Ask God to help you.

MOSTLY 4s You're pretty kind to others, but you can still improve.

MOSTLY 5s Congratulations! You show God's love and care to others.

THINGS TO DO

☐ Apologize to someone you've been unkind to.

☐ Do something kind for someone who has been unkind to you.

☐ Memorize a verse on kindness, such as Luke 6:31 or Galatians 5:14. Repeat it to yourself before responding when you've been mistreated.

☐ Ask God to help you consistently treat all people the way you'd want to be treated.

THINGS TO REMEMBER

We prove ourselves by our purity, our understanding, our patience, our kindness, by the Holy Spirit within us, and by our sincere love.
2 CORINTHIANS 6:6

Three things will last forever—faith, hope, and love—and the greatest of these is love.
1 CORINTHIANS 13:13

Do everything with love. **1 CORINTHIANS 16:14**

The whole law can be summed up in this one command: "Love your neighbor as yourself."
GALATIANS 5:14

Above all, clothe yourselves with love, which binds us all together in perfect harmony. **COLOSSIANS 3:14**

We have committed the Golden Rule to memory; let us now commit it to life.
EDWIN MARKHAM

I am a little pencil in the hand of a writing God, who is sending a love letter to the world.
MOTHER TERESA

No kind action ever stops with itself. One kind action leads to another.
AMELIA EARHART

What's Mine Is Mine

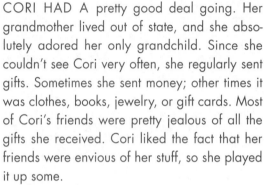

CORI HAD A pretty good deal going. Her grandmother lived out of state, and she absolutely adored her only grandchild. Since she couldn't see Cori very often, she regularly sent gifts. Sometimes she sent money; other times it was clothes, books, jewelry, or gift cards. Most of Cori's friends were pretty jealous of all the gifts she received. Cori liked the fact that her friends were envious of her stuff, so she played it up some.

One night a group of friends had a sleepover. Cori came to the party with a big bag of candy she had bought with money from her grandmother. Chocolates, lollipops, jelly beans—any kind of candy you could think of was in her pink paper bag. As the group talked and played games, Cori munched on her candy and made a big deal about how good it was. Finally Melissa said, "Hey, Cori, can I have piece of chocolate?" Cori's response: "No way!" The rest of the night no one said a word to Cori. She had her candy all to herself . . . and not one friend to bother her.

Selfishness makes no friends. It wasn't the candy itself that was a big deal; it was Cori's attitude about it. She was just being plain old stingy. She had more than enough candy to enjoy herself and also share with her friends. Cori's behavior did not follow the way Jesus taught us to treat other people. The Bible says that if you have two shirts and someone else doesn't have any, then you should give that person one of yours (Luke 3:11). Jesus said to love others as you love yourself. The way Cori showed off by bringing a big bag of candy *not* to share certainly didn't model that kind of love. It might give her a perspective check to see the way Jesus treated others so she can learn to do the same.

CHECKUP TIME

On a scale of 1 to 5, how good are you at sharing?

1 = never
2 = not very often
3 = sometimes
4 = most of the time
5 = always

I'm happy to share what I have with others.
1   2   3   4   5

I try to put others before myself, as Jesus did.
1   2   3   4   5

When I see someone who has very little, I find something I can share with him or her.
1   2   3   4   5

I celebrate with my friends when they get something new or succeed.
1   2   3   4   5

My friends are more important than my stuff.
1   2   3   4   5

KEY

MOSTLY 1s Uh-oh, you'd better choose one area from the statements above to begin working on.

MOSTLY 2s There is definitely room for improvement.

MOSTLY 3s Right in the middle. You can definitely be more generous.

MOSTLY 4s You're not the stingiest person ever, but you can still improve.

MOSTLY 5s Congratulations! You are generous and caring.

THINGS TO DO

☐ Deliberately share something of yours one time each week.

☐ Write down your favorite things about your friends, and then make a list of your favorite stuff. Compare the two lists, and ask God to help you make people a bigger priority.

☐ Ask forgiveness from anyone you've hurt because you didn't share.

☐ Find a way to help someone who has less than you do. You might want to donate clothes or toys, host a fund-raiser, or choose a charity to give money to.

THINGS TO REMEMBER

If someone has enough money to live well and sees a brother or sister in need but shows no compassion—how can God's love be in that person? **1 JOHN 3:17**

Don't be selfish; don't try to impress others. Be humble, thinking of others as better than yourselves. **PHILIPPIANS 2:3**

They share freely and give generously to those in need. Their good deeds will be remembered forever. They will have influence and honor. **PSALM 112:9**

Blessed are those who are generous, because they feed the poor. **PROVERBS 22:9**

Tell them to use their money to do good. They should be rich in good works and generous to those in need, always being ready to share with others. **1 TIMOTHY 6:18**

There is no delight in owning anything unshared.
SENECA

Think of giving not as a duty but as a privilege.
JOHN D. ROCKEFELLER JR.

What do we live for, if it is not to make life less difficult to each other?
GEORGE ELIOT,
FROM *MIDDLEMARCH*

It Hurts So Much

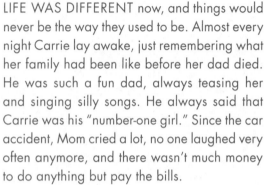

Even when I walk through the darkest valley, I will not be afraid, for you are close beside me. Your rod and your staff protect and comfort me.
PSALM 23:4

LIFE WAS DIFFERENT now, and things would never be the way they used to be. Almost every night Carrie lay awake, just remembering what her family had been like before her dad died. He was such a fun dad, always teasing her and singing silly songs. He always said that Carrie was his "number-one girl." Since the car accident, Mom cried a lot, no one laughed very often anymore, and there wasn't much money to do anything but pay the bills.

Carrie didn't understand why God would take her dad away. If God loved her the way her youth group leader and pastor said he did, then why would he let this happen? She didn't want to go to church or sing songs or read her Bible anymore. And she definitely did not want to pray. It felt like God had betrayed her.

There's no denying it—sometimes it's hard to understand why things happen. In the midst of painful times, it can be hard to believe that God still cares. But even when it doesn't feel like it or when things happen that don't make sense, God still loves you. He hurts when you hurt. That's what people do when they love someone. The fact that we live in a sinful, imperfect world means that sometimes painful things happen. It doesn't mean God doesn't love you or care about what you're going through. If you can hold on to him through the pain, you'll be able to see so many ways he shows his love in the midst of every painful thing you go through. Trust his love.

CHECKUP TIME

On a scale of 1 to 5, how much do you believe in God's love?

1 = never
2 = not very often
3 = sometimes
4 = most of the time
5 = always

I believe that God has a good plan, even when things are painful or don't make sense.
1   2   3   4   5

When I'm hurting, I let others encourage and support me.
1   2   3   4   5

I read the Bible and pray to find support and help.
1   2   3   4   5

When I'm angry or sad, I'm honest with God about how I'm feeling.
1   2   3   4   5

I believe God loves me, even when I can't feel it.
1   2   3   4   5

KEY

MOSTLY 1s You must be really hurting. Choose one thing to begin working on to find encouragement and help.

MOSTLY 2s It sounds like you have a hard time believing in God's love. Keep working on trusting him.

MOSTLY 3s Average. But God's love is *not* average. Keep seeking him.

MOSTLY 4s You're doing pretty well. Keep going.

MOSTLY 5s You know how to handle pain and grief in a healthy way.

THINGS TO DO

☐ Write a letter to God and tell him why you're hurting so much. Be honest. He will understand.

☐ Make a list of all the things God has given you just today.

☐ Talk to someone about how you're feeling about a difficult situation—perhaps a family member or a leader at your church.

☐ Memorize a verse about how much God loves you, such as 1 Peter 5:7 or Romans 8:28.

THINGS TO REMEMBER

God loved the world so much that he gave his one and only Son, so that everyone who believes in him will not perish but have eternal life. **JOHN 3:16**

Give all your worries and cares to God, for he cares about you. **1 PETER 5:7**

The LORD is close to all who call on him, yes, to all who call on him in truth. **PSALM 145:18**

We know that God causes everything to work together for the good of those who love God and are called according to his purpose for them. **ROMANS 8:28**

God is love, and all who live in love live in God, and God lives in them. **1 JOHN 4:16**

God is even kinder than you think.
SAINT THERESA

Sorrow looks back.
Worry looks around.
Faith looks up.
UNKNOWN

There is a seed of God's love in every event, every circumstance, every unpleasant situation in which you may find yourself.
BARBARA JOHNSON

Heart-Stopping Fear

SOME NIGHTS NICOLE could hardly sleep. Her mind kept racing with all the possibilities of terrible things that could happen. After a while it felt like her heart was about to stop because she was so afraid. Sometimes she got so scared that she couldn't get a deep breath and she broke out in a cold sweat. Her brother Ethan was in the marines, and it seemed like he was always sent to the most dangerous places.

Nicole was terrified that something awful was going to happen to him. When he left for boot camp, Nicole cried and cried. The fear started then, and it had only gotten worse since. Now, each time she saw the news on TV or read the headlines online, she quickly scanned for news from overseas. She just didn't know what she would do if something happened to Ethan. She didn't know how her mom would react either, and that scared her almost as much.

There's no doubt about it—the world is a scary place these days. It seems like people have become experts at ways to hurt other people. If you let your mind dwell on what might happen, you'll live in fear most of the time.

The antidote or prescription for fear is trust—trust that there is someone in charge of what's happening in the world, someone who can protect you and your loved ones. That someone is God. Yeah, bad things do happen. People hurt other people, and sometimes people we love

get hurt, or worse. Sometimes we don't understand why God doesn't stop the bad things, but he never leaves us to go through them alone. He walks beside us, helping us through the pain. The best way to stop that paralyzing fear is to ask God to take care of whatever you're afraid of. Give it to him, then trust him to handle it.

CHECKUP TIME

On a scale of 1 to 5, how are you doing in the trust area?

1 = never
2 = not very often
3 = sometimes
4 = most of the time
5 = always

I trust that God is big enough to handle whatever I'm going through.

1   2   3   4   5

I keep my fears in check.

1   2   3   4   5

I believe that God is always with me, even if I feel alone sometimes.

1   2   3   4   5

I ask God to help me when I'm afraid.

1   2   3   4   5

When I'm scared I look back and remember times God has helped me before.

1   2   3   4   5

KEY

MOSTLY 1s Whoa, you'd better read this devo again and take an honest look at your "trustitude."

MOSTLY 2s You've taken some baby steps to trusting. Keep moving in the right direction.

MOSTLY 3s Average is the best we can say. Talk to someone about your fears.

MOSTLY 4s You're showing some real maturity here. Good job.

MOSTLY 5s Excellent! You've learned the lesson of trust very well.

THINGS TO DO

☐ Take a baby step toward trusting. Choose to trust God with one little thing. Give it to him and leave it there.

☐ Keep a prayer journal. Write down your requests and God's answers to help you remember the ways God has been faithful in your life.

☐ Choose a verse about trusting God, such as Joshua 1:9 or Proverbs 3:5. Write it down and read it every day.

☐ Tell someone what you're afraid of. Ask that person to pray with you about it.

THINGS TO REMEMBER

Those who know your name trust in you, for you, O LORD, do not abandon those who search for you. **PSALM 9:10**

The LORD is my strength and shield. I trust him with all my heart. He helps me, and my heart is filled with joy. I burst out in songs of thanksgiving. **PSALM 28:7**

Trust in the LORD with all your heart; do not depend on your own understanding. **PROVERBS 3:5**

Those who trust in the LORD will find new strength. They will soar high on wings like eagles. They will run and not grow weary. They will walk and not faint. **ISAIAH 40:31**

Don't let your hearts be troubled. Trust in God, and trust also in me. **JOHN 14:1**

Fear can keep us up all night long, but faith makes one fine pillow.
PHILIP GULLEY

Worry gives a small thing a big shadow.
SWEDISH PROVERB

The only known cure for fear is faith.
LENA KELLOGG SADLER

Not Good Enough

"I DIDN'T MAKE IT. I'm not even good enough for the B team." Keri looked at the list of girls who had made the volleyball team. Her name wasn't on it. Even though she had practiced serves and bumps every day and she desperately wanted to be on the team, she hadn't made it.

Just then Keri heard some other girls coming to check out the list on the bulletin board. They were laughing and talking, confident their names would be on the list. Keri recognized most of their voices and quickly glanced at the bulletin board. It looked like they'd all made the team. They belonged together, and she didn't.

You're not good enough. The words weren't spoken out loud, but Keri felt like they might as well have been. Anyway, it was true. She wasn't good enough . . . at anything. *I'm just a loser. Not even good enough for the B team,* Keri thought. She grabbed her backpack and ran down the hall. She didn't want to be there when the other girls came. It felt like their names were flashing in congratulatory neon lights, while a loudspeaker was announcing, "KERI ISN'T GOOD ENOUGH!"

Disappointment is tough, isn't it? How do you handle it when you want something very much but it doesn't happen? You can listen to that voice that keeps telling you that you're not good enough (probably Satan's voice, by the way), or you can accept the situation and look for the next opportunity. Remember, God made you. He made you just the way he wants you to be. He has stuff for you to do—stuff you're good at. It may not be volleyball or orchestra or whatever your best friend is good at, but there is something.

Do you need some examples? Okay, some people are good at being true-blue, loyal friends or listening to others' problems. Some are good helpers to their neighbors or to the elderly. Some are good at babysitting or taking care of animals. Some are good writers or singers. Stop and think about it. You're good at something. Concentrate on that and thank God for making you . . . *you!*

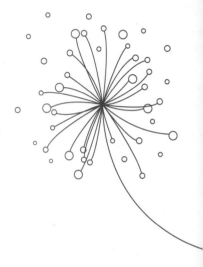

CHECKUP TIME

On a scale of 1 to 5, how are you doing when it comes to self-confidence?

1 = never
2 = not very often
3 = sometimes
4 = most of the time
5 = always

I can ignore that inside voice that says I'm not good enough.

1   2   3   4   5

I believe God made me special just the way I am.

1   2   3   4   5

I appreciate the abilities and talents God has given me.

1   2   3   4   5

I bounce back from disappointment quickly.

1   2   3   4   5

I encourage my friends to find what they're good at and pursue it.

1   2   3   4   5

KEY

MOSTLY 1s Whoa, you'd better read this devo again and start changing your self-talk.

MOSTLY 2s You're working at self-confidence. Keep learning.

MOSTLY 3s Not bad, but God wants you to be even more comfortable with who he made you to be.

MOSTLY 4s You're showing confidence in who God made you to be. Good job.

MOSTLY 5s Excellent! You've got healthy self-confidence.

THINGS TO DO

☐ Look at your answers to the statements on the previous page. Choose one area to work on this week.

☐ Make a list of the things you are good at and enjoy doing.

☐ Think about something you'd like to learn how to do and take the first step toward pursuing it.

☐ Thank God for making you just the way he wants you to be.

THINGS TO REMEMBER

God created human beings in his own image. In the image of God he created them; male and female he created them. **GENESIS 1:27**

Not a single sparrow can fall to the ground without your Father knowing it. . . . You are more valuable to God than a whole flock of sparrows. **MATTHEW 10:29, 31**

In his grace, God has given us different gifts for doing certain things well. **ROMANS 12:6**

God has given each of you a gift from his great variety of spiritual gifts. Use them well to serve one another. **1 PETER 4:10**

All of you together are Christ's body, and each of you is a part of it. **1 CORINTHIANS 12:27**

Sometimes when I consider what tremendous consequences come from little things . . . I am tempted to think there are no little things.
BRUCE BARTON

You gain strength, courage, and confidence by every experience in which you really stop to look fear in the face. . . . You must do the thing which you think you cannot do.
ELEANOR ROOSEVELT

Be who you are and say what you feel, because those who mind don't matter and those who matter don't mind.
DR. SEUSS

It's Not My Fault!

"I DIDN'T GET my homework done because the electricity went out at our house and I couldn't use the computer," Allie told her teacher. She sounded truly sorry that this had happened. She should, since she had been thinking about what excuse she could give ever since 9:30 the night before!

"Yeah," said Michael, who lived two doors down from Allie, "the electricity went out, but not until 9:30!" If angry looks could hurt someone, Michael would be in the hospital right now. Allie's teacher crossed her arms and waited to hear what Allie would say now.

Allie's mind raced to find another excuse for not finishing her homework . . . her arm was broken? No, that obviously wasn't true. Umm, she had a sudden onset of the two-hour flu? No, that probably wouldn't work either. *Come on*, she thought. *I have to come up with something!*

How about the truth, Allie? Here's the thing: Allie has a problem. She always has an excuse for everything. When something goes wrong or when she doesn't do something she's supposed to do, it's never her fault. She always has an excuse as to why she didn't follow through. Allie doesn't accept responsibility for her own mistakes or choices. In the case of her homework, she didn't get it done simply because she was sending messages to her friends until

9:30. After that, the electricity did go out and she had a problem.

Of course, Allie has come up with excuses so often that no one believes her anymore. Not even her teacher. So she's not fooling anyone except herself. Allie has done the "it's not my fault" thing for so long that she actually believes it now. What Allie doesn't understand is that everyone messes up sometimes and that's okay. There are lots of stories in the Bible of good people who made mistakes. God always gave them another chance, and he will do the same for Allie—and for you. So what's the best way to handle it when you mess up? Admit it. Learn from it. Apologize and accept the consequences, then move on. Simple, huh?

CHECKUP TIME

On a scale of 1 to 5, how are you doing when it comes to making excuses?

1 = never
2 = not very often
3 = sometimes
4 = most of the time
5 = always

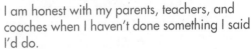

I take responsibility for my actions—good or bad.

1   2   3   4   5

I apologize for my actions when necessary.

1   2   3   4   5

I use my time wisely so I don't really need to make excuses.

1   2   3   4   5

I follow through on my commitments.

1   2   3   4   5

I am honest with my parents, teachers, and coaches when I haven't done something I said I'd do.

1   2   3   4   5

KEY

MOSTLY 1s Stop! You should read this devo again—no excuses!

MOSTLY 2s You've got a ways to go, but at least you have a start.

MOSTLY 3s Okay—average—but you can do better.

MOSTLY 4s You're showing some real honesty here. Good job.

MOSTLY 5s Excellent! No excuses needed here!

THINGS TO DO

☐ How did you do on the "no excuses" quiz? Decide which action you need to work on the most and begin to make one change this week.

☐ Make a list of things you most often make excuses about.

☐ Ask a friend to hold you accountable to always tell the truth.

☐ Next time you're tempted to lie, tell the truth instead. Write down the date and keep track of each time you block a lie. See if it gets easier to tell the truth each time.

THINGS TO REMEMBER

I [God] judge each of you according to your deeds. EZEKIEL 33:20

What joy for those whose record the LORD has cleared of guilt, whose lives are lived in complete honesty! PSALM 32:2

Teach me your ways, O LORD, that I may live according to your truth! Grant me purity of heart, so that I may honor you. PSALM 86:11

Honesty guides good people; dishonesty destroys treacherous people. PROVERBS 11:3

Our actions will show that we belong to the truth, so we will be confident when we stand before God. 1 JOHN 3:19

He that is good for making excuses is seldom good for anything else.
BENJAMIN FRANKLIN

To keep your feet on the ground, carry some responsibility on your shoulders.
UNKNOWN

God gives every bird its food, but he does not throw it into the nest.
J. G. HOLLAND

Broken Dreams

"STOP IT! STOP laughing. Stop talking. Stop acting like everything is all right!" That's what Charlotte wanted to scream at everyone around her. She didn't, though—that would take way too much energy. It made Charlotte angry to see other people acting as if life were completely normal. Her mom and dad were getting a divorce. Dad had already moved out, and Charlotte hardly ever saw him. She missed him. She even missed all the arguing and fighting her parents used to do. At least they were all home together then. The truth was, Charlotte was scared. How would she and Mom have enough money? Who would fix things that broke around the house? Who would help her with her math homework or come to her soccer games? What if she never saw her dad anymore? It felt like her world had broken into pieces.

Divorce stinks. That's about the best thing you can say about it. And the ones who can be hurt the most are the kids, who are torn between their parents. In the best situations the mom and dad work together to make things as easy as possible for the whole family. But that doesn't always happen. So what do you do?

Remember that if your mom and dad no longer live together, that doesn't mean either of them will stop loving you. Also remember that it is not your fault if your parents get a divorce. It doesn't matter how disobedient or crabby or stubborn you have ever been—that is *not* why your parents couldn't work out their problems. You may always miss your family being the way it used to be, but the pain won't always be as intense as it is now. Finally, remember that God will walk with you through this hard time. He loves you completely, and nothing will ever take that away.

CHECKUP TIME

On a scale of 1 to 5, how are you doing at handling your feelings?

1 = never
2 = not very often
3 = sometimes
4 = most of the time
5 = always

When I'm angry, I calmly discuss it with the person I am angry with.

1   2   3   4   5

I know that my parents' problems are not my fault.

1   2   3   4   5

My actions are controlled by godly decisions, not emotions.

1   2   3   4   5

I give my problems to God and leave them there.

1   2   3   4   5

I forgive people who hurt me or make me angry.

1   2   3   4   5

KEY

MOSTLY 1s You might want to talk to an adult you trust about ways to handle your feelings.

MOSTLY 2s Your emotions are controlling you—time to do something about it.

MOSTLY 3s Average, but you can do better.

MOSTLY 4s Not bad. You're doing pretty well.

MOSTLY 5s Hooray! You are doing great at handling your emotions.

THINGS TO DO

☐ If you scored mostly 1s or 2s on the quiz, choose one statement to work on.

☐ Make a list of where your anger or hurt comes from.

☐ Talk with someone who could help you understand your anger or hurt.

☐ Memorize a verse about controlling your emotions, such as Psalm 4:4 or James 1:20.

THINGS TO REMEMBER

No power in the sky above or in the earth below—indeed, nothing in all creation will ever be able to separate us from the love of God that is revealed in Christ Jesus our Lord. ROMANS 8:39

People with understanding control their anger. PROVERBS 14:29

You bless the godly, O LORD; you surround them with your shield of love. PSALM 5:12

Human anger does not produce the righteousness God desires. JAMES 1:20

Don't sin by letting anger control you. Think about it overnight and remain silent. PSALM 4:4

We cannot learn without pain.
ARISTOTLE

God whispers to us in our pleasures, speaks to us in our conscience, but shouts in our pains: It is His megaphone to rouse a deaf world.
C. S. LEWIS

Love doesn't make the world go round. Love is what makes the ride worthwhile.
FRANKLIN P. JONES

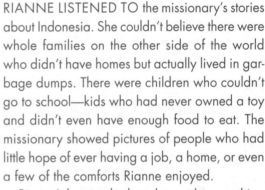

I Can't . . .

RIANNE LISTENED TO the missionary's stories about Indonesia. She couldn't believe there were whole families on the other side of the world who didn't have homes but actually lived in garbage dumps. There were children who couldn't go to school—kids who had never owned a toy and didn't even have enough food to eat. The missionary showed pictures of people who had little hope of ever having a job, a home, or even a few of the comforts Rianne enjoyed.

Rianne's heart ached, and more than anything she wanted to do something to help these people. Several ideas raced through her mind. She could try to raise some money for the families. She could collect toys or food or . . . well, there had to be something she could do! But even though Rianne felt compassion for the children, she thought, *I'm just one person, and I'm not smart enough to organize a group to do anything. I wish I could help, but I could never get other people to listen to me and work with me. I give up.*

Lack of self-confidence is crippling. It can come from feeling you must have gotten in the wrong line when talents and stuff like that were handed out. The flip side of low self-confidence is being filled with pride. That's not good either. But somewhere in the middle is having a healthy opinion of yourself. That opinion is based on a trust that God knew exactly what he was doing when he made you, just as you are.

The Bible promises that God will give you the strength, energy, and ideas to carry out the work he gives you to do. Low self-confidence keeps you from trying new things and using the abilities you have. It cheats you out of sharing in God's work in the world. Responding to opportunities with "I can't" is disrespectful to God himself because that attitude questions what kind of job God did when he made you. Come on, no more "I can't." Replace it with "I'll try!"

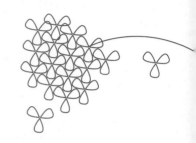

CHECKUP TIME

On a scale of 1 to 5, how are you doing at tackling new challenges?

1 = never
2 = not very often
3 = sometimes
4 = most of the time
5 = always

I am confident in the abilities God has given me.
1   2   3   4   5

I believe God will help me do any work he calls me to do.
1   2   3   4   5

I am willing to try new things.
1   2   3   4   5

I enjoy working hard at a project.
1   2   3   4   5

I learn from my failures.
1   2   3   4   5

KEY

MOSTLY 1s You don't believe in yourself much.

MOSTLY 2s Are you remembering that God's strength will help you?

MOSTLY 3s Average, but God made you better than average!

MOSTLY 4s Not bad. You're getting there!

MOSTLY 5s Hurray! You trust God's strength and help in your life!

THINGS TO DO

☐ Choose one thing from the quiz on the previous page to concentrate on.

☐ Memorize 2 Corinthians 12:9, which tells about God's help. Write it down and place it somewhere you can see it every day.

☐ With a friend, write down ten new things you'd like to try someday. Each week, decide on one of those new adventures you'd like to tackle together.

☐ Next time you hear someone say, "I can't . . ." remind that person of something he or she *can* do.

THINGS TO REMEMBER

Search for the LORD and for his strength; continually seek him. **PSALM 105:4**

With God's help we will do mighty things, for he will trample down our foes. **PSALM 108:13**

He trains my hands for battle; he strengthens my arm to draw a bronze bow. **2 SAMUEL 22:35**

The Holy Spirit helps us in our weakness. **ROMANS 8:26**

I can do everything through Christ, who gives me strength. **PHILIPPIANS 4:13**

The greatest test of courage on earth is to bear defeat without losing heart.
ROBERT G. INGERSOLL

The greatest barrier to success is the fear of failure.
SVEN-GÖRAN ERIKSSON

I more fear what is within me than what comes from without.
MARTIN LUTHER

Sucked In

SAM LOOKED UP just as her bedroom clock flipped to 1:30 a.m. *Wow, it's going to be hard to get up tomorrow,* she thought. For just a minute she considered going to bed, but then her computer beeped that she had another message, and she forgot all about sleep again. Sam would never admit it, but she was addicted to her computer. She spent every spare minute online. She couldn't help herself. When she was doing anything else, her mind wandered back to the computer, and she wondered who might be online at that very moment and what they were talking about. Her addiction had gotten so bad that her grades were slipping and she was often in trouble with her parents. She seldom went anywhere or read a book or played with her puppy. The only thing she wanted to do was to be online.

It is not easy to keep a balance in your life. It's wonderful when you find something you really enjoy doing. But when it starts to take over your life, you may need to check your priorities. There are things you need to do every day, responsibilities at home and school and with your friends and family. If something becomes such an addiction that you aren't getting those other things done, there is a problem.

Some people allow addictions to control their lives, and that starts a snowball of problems. Sometimes small addictions like the Internet can

lead to bigger addictions that might be more dangerous and have damaging consequences. One way to stop addictions is by making sure there is variety in how you spend your time. It's also wise to fulfill your responsibilities before doing things that are just for fun. Ask God to give you the strength to do this. He may help you tackle this just between you and him, or he may guide you to a friend, parent, teacher, or leader at your church who can talk with you and help you control anything that is addictive in your life.

CHECKUP TIME

On a scale of 1 to 5, how wisely do you spend your time?

1 = never
2 = not very often
3 = sometimes
4 = most of the time
5 = always

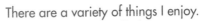

I finish my responsibilities before doing things that are just for fun.
1   2   3   4   5

I manage my time well.
1   2   3   4   5

I keep a good balance between what I have to do and what I want to do.
1   2   3   4   5

There are a variety of things I enjoy.
1   2   3   4   5

I finish my chores and homework on time.
1   2   3   4   5

KEY

MOSTLY 1s Yikes, how do you ever get anything done?

MOSTLY 2s It sounds like you need some help with time management!

MOSTLY 3s Right in the middle, with room for improvement.

MOSTLY 4s Pretty good!

MOSTLY 5s Hurray! You are doing great at balancing your life!

THINGS TO DO

- ☐ If you didn't circle all fives above, choose one thing to work on to balance your life more.

- ☐ Ask a parent or friend if he or she thinks you have a problem with addictions.

- ☐ Keep a chart of how you spend your time for two days.

- ☐ Ask God to help you be more balanced in your life.

THINGS TO REMEMBER

You have given me your shield of victory. Your right hand supports me; your help has made me great. **PSALM 18:35**

LORD, remind me how brief my time on earth will be. Remind me that my days are numbered—how fleeting my life is. **PSALM 39:4**

I hold you by your right hand—I, the LORD your God. And I say to you, "Don't be afraid. I am here to help you." **ISAIAH 41:13**

Sin is no longer your master, for you no longer live under the requirements of the law. Instead, you live under the freedom of God's grace. **ROMANS 6:14**

[Christ] gave his life to purchase freedom for everyone. This is the message God gave to the world at just the right time. **1 TIMOTHY 2:6**

Time is free, but it's priceless. You can't own it, but you can use it. You can't keep it, but you can spend it. Once you've lost it, you can never get it back.
HARVEY MACKAY

How we spend our days is, of course, how we spend our lives.
ANNIE DILLARD

Right now counts forever.
R. C. SPROUL

Let the Earth Swallow Me

IF LINDSEY COULD have controlled the universe at that moment, she would have had the earth open up and swallow her, taking her far away from everyone who was watching her right then. A wave of warmth crept up her neck and across her face. She knew her face was red, and she could feel beads of perspiration popping out on her upper lip. *Why do things like this happen to me?* Lindsey wondered.

It was an honor to be asked to lead the Pledge of Allegiance over the school loudspeaker. Only eighth graders got to do it, and only certain students were given the chance. So when Lindsey was given the opportunity, she felt special. She didn't worry too much about it beforehand; after all, everyone knows the Pledge of Allegiance, right? Whether it was nerves or whatever, Lindsey got about six words into the Pledge and then her mind went completely blank. The rest of the Pledge never came into her mind, and it seemed like thirty minutes passed before she could think of anything else to say. It was really only a few seconds. Lindsey could hear some of the other eighth graders giggling. She wished she could suddenly be invisible!

Have you ever been embarrassed? It's awful, isn't it? You can get really down on yourself when you are embarrassed about something if you let yourself think about it too long. And then there are those people who like to give you a hard time about it. They jump at the opportunity to tease you mercilessly—and these people may even be your friends!

But think about it—is any person perfect? Nope, everyone makes mistakes sometimes. And circumstances beyond our control happen sometimes. So everyone is embarrassed once in a while. You might not be able to prevent embarrassment, but you can control how you react. Don't take yourself too seriously—remember that you belong to God and that he is never embarrassed to call you his daughter. Learn to laugh at your mistakes, and then go on with life.

CHECKUP TIME

On a scale of 1 to 5, how do you handle embarrassment?

1 = never
2 = not very often
3 = sometimes
4 = most of the time
5 = always

I can laugh at my mistakes.
1   2   3   4   5

I encourage my friends when they are embarrassed, instead of laughing at them.
1   2   3   4   5

When I mess up, I try, try again.
1   2   3   4   5

I learn something when I fail.
1   2   3   4   5

I am willing to try new things, even if it means I could mess up.
1   2   3   4   5

KEY

MOSTLY 1s Uh-oh. You're pretty worried about what people think about you.

MOSTLY 2s Not too courageous, are you?

MOSTLY 3s You're doing average.

MOSTLY 4s Pretty good!

MOSTLY 5s You're a courageous risk taker. Good for you!

THINGS TO DO

☐ What did you learn from the quiz on the previous page? Choose one area of your life to work on developing courage in, and be willing to fail once in a while.

☐ Be sensitive when others fail or make a mistake. Encourage them to see the lighter side of the situation.

☐ Ask God to help you not take yourself so seriously.

☐ Next time you mess up in front of others, be the first to laugh at yourself.

THINGS TO REMEMBER

The LORD is my strength and my song; he has given me victory. This is my God, and I will praise him—my father's God, and I will exalt him! **EXODUS 15:2**

Be strong and courageous, all you who put your hope in the LORD! **PSALM 31:24**

Be strong and courageous! Do not be afraid and do not panic before them. For the LORD your God will personally go ahead of you. He will neither fail you nor abandon you. **DEUTERONOMY 31:6**

Make allowance for each other's faults, and forgive anyone who offends you. Remember, the Lord forgave you, so you must forgive others.
COLOSSIANS 3:13

God has not given us a spirit of fear and timidity, but of power, love, and self-discipline.
2 TIMOTHY 1:7

All serious daring starts from within.
EUDORA WELTY

Courage is going from failure to failure without losing enthusiasm.
WINSTON CHURCHILL

The grass is greener on the other side of the fence. It's just as hard to chew. You've got to mow it, too. It's just different grass.
BOB SMITH

I ♥ My Friends

The seeds of good deeds become a tree of life; a wise person wins friends.
PROVERBS 11:30

ERICA WAS SO excited. Her house had become the official friend hangout. Of course she and her friends didn't call it that. But her mom said everyone could come over for a giant sleepover. She even baked cookies for them and promised to make pancakes for breakfast. All of Erica's best friends were coming. There would be eight of them, plus Erica. They were going to play games and eat pizza and listen to music and talk and laugh all night long! There wouldn't be much sleep at this sleepover.

This group of nine girls had been friends for a long time. They all met in a park district class. They didn't go to the same schools or even the same church. But they made sure they stayed friends. Erica loved each one of them for a different reason. Julia could always make her laugh. Sarah listened to her problems and kept them a secret. Jamie showed her new ways to do her hair . . . and on and on. They all thought the same things were funny, and they liked a lot of the same things. It was so much fun to be together!

Friends are a great treasure, aren't they? Good friends help you through the hard times and celebrate the good times with you. Of course, family is important too, but you don't get to choose who your family is. Friends are people you meet and then choose to get to know.

God knew that friendships would make our lives a lot more fun. Remember that friendship is a two-way street. You may have good friends, but it's important to *be* a good friend too. Friends give you their time, concern, and care, and you give all of that right back to them. Friends give each other the benefit of the doubt when there is a problem. Friends talk over things before little arguments turn into big fights. Friends help whenever they can; they stand up for each other, they pray for each other, and they just celebrate life together!

CHECKUP TIME

On a scale of 1 to 5, how good of a friend are you?

1 = never
2 = not very often
3 = sometimes
4 = most of the time
5 = always

I thank God for my friends.

1 2 3 4 5

I tell my friends how much I appreciate them.

1 2 3 4 5

I am loyal to my friends.

1 2 3 4 5

I help my friends when they have problems.

1 2 3 4 5

I let my friends help me when I need it.

1 2 3 4 5

KEY

MOSTLY 1s Whoa, if you're not careful, you won't have any friends!

MOSTLY 2s You need to do some work in the friendship department.

MOSTLY 3s You are a so-so friend.

MOSTLY 4s You appreciate your friends.

MOSTLY 5s You are an awesome friend!

THINGS TO DO

☐ If you didn't get mostly 4s or 5s on the quiz, choose one statement to begin working on right away.

☐ Think about one thing you appreciate about each of your friends; then share those things with your friends.

☐ Write down some ways you can be a better friend this week.

☐ Pray for one of your friends each day.

THINGS TO REMEMBER

Jonathan made David reaffirm his vow of friendship again, for Jonathan loved David as he loved himself.
1 SAMUEL 20:17

The LORD is a friend to those who fear him. He teaches them his covenant. **PSALM 25:14**

Every time I think of you, I give thanks to my God.
PHILIPPIANS 1:3

This is the message you have heard from the beginning: We should love one another.
1 JOHN 3:11

Love each other deeply with all your heart.
1 PETER 1:22

If I could give you a gift, my friend, I'd give you the ability to see yourself as others see you, so you would know how very special you are.
UNKNOWN

Friends are those rare people who ask how we are and then wait to hear the answer.
ED CUNNINGHAM

Friendship is a very Comforting sort of Thing.
WINNIE THE POOH

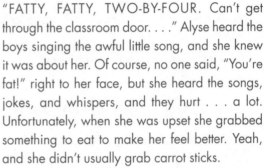

Getting off the Couch

"FATTY, FATTY, TWO-BY-FOUR. Can't get through the classroom door. . . ." Alyse heard the boys singing the awful little song, and she knew it was about her. Of course, no one said, "You're fat!" right to her face, but she heard the songs, jokes, and whispers, and they hurt . . . a lot. Unfortunately, when she was upset she grabbed something to eat to make her feel better. Yeah, and she didn't usually grab carrot sticks.

In some ways being overweight made Alyse feel invisible to the rest of the world. No one seemed to respect her opinion, and people didn't invite her to do things with them. It was like she didn't matter since she was fat. But of course, she was anything *but* invisible when it came to the jokes and mean comments. It wasn't like she hadn't tried to lose weight. She had gone on plenty of diets, but she never had much success.

There is no excuse for making fun of someone, whether because of her weight or for another reason. A girl who is overweight might feel discouraged because she wants to be healthier, and she might find some tasks more challenging because of her weight. Mean comments from others only make things worse.

It's important to remember that even if you're overweight, you are still a valuable person with a kind heart, a good sense of humor, various talents, and lots to offer the world. God made your body, and he loves you just the way you are. He also wants you to do a good job taking care of the body he has given you. When you realize that you are a creation of God, it will make a difference in the way you see other people—and yourself!

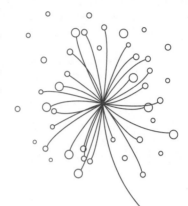

CHECKUP TIME

On a scale of 1 to 5, how are you doing at taking care of yourself?

1 = never
2 = not very often
3 = sometimes
4 = most of the time
5 = always

I stay away from junk food.
1   2   3   4   5

I get some kind of exercise every day.
1   2   3   4   5

I get enough sleep each night.
1   2   3   4   5

I am kind to all people, including those who are overweight.
1   2   3   4   5

I encourage my friends to take care of their bodies.
1   2   3   4   5

KEY

MOSTLY 1s Whoa! You need to make some serious changes for your health.

MOSTLY 2s You have some work to do.

MOSTLY 3s Right in the middle—not bad, but not great either.

MOSTLY 4s There's still room for improvement.

MOSTLY 5s You are physically fit and healthy!

THINGS TO DO

☐ If you didn't mark all 5s on the previous page, choose one area—diet, exercise, sleep, or encouragement—to begin working on.

☐ Keep a food and exercise diary to find ways you can be healthier.

☐ Get an exercise buddy—find a friend to walk, jog, or ride your bike with.

☐ Thank God for the body he gave you.

THINGS TO REMEMBER

In my distress I cried out to the LORD; yes, I cried to my God for help. He heard me from his sanctuary; my cry reached his ears. **2 SAMUEL 22:7**

The LORD gives his people strength. The LORD blesses them with peace. **PSALM 29:11**

A peaceful heart leads to a healthy body. **PROVERBS 14:30**

Do you like honey? Don't eat too much, or it will make you sick! **PROVERBS 25:16**

Do not let any part of your body become an instrument of evil to serve sin. Instead, give yourselves completely to God. **ROMANS 6:13**

By swallowing evil words unsaid, no one has ever harmed his stomach.
WINSTON CHURCHILL

Action may not always bring happiness; but there is no happiness without action.
BENJAMIN DISRAELI

Parties who want milk should not seat themselves on a stool in the middle of the field in hope that the cow will back up to them.
ELBERT HUBBARD

Good Job, God!

Sing praises to God, sing praises; sing praises to our King, sing praises!
PSALM 47:6

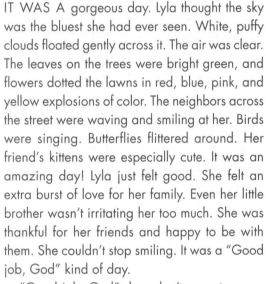

IT WAS A gorgeous day. Lyla thought the sky was the bluest she had ever seen. White, puffy clouds floated gently across it. The air was clear. The leaves on the trees were bright green, and flowers dotted the lawns in red, blue, pink, and yellow explosions of color. The neighbors across the street were waving and smiling at her. Birds were singing. Butterflies flittered around. Her friend's kittens were especially cute. It was an amazing day! Lyla just felt good. She felt an extra burst of love for her family. Even her little brother wasn't irritating her too much. She was thankful for her friends and happy to be with them. She couldn't stop smiling. It was a "Good job, God" kind of day.

"Good job, God" days don't seem to come often enough, do they? Those are the days when it seems like all the puzzle pieces fit and everything in your life is going smoothly. Your family is getting along. Your schoolwork is going well. Your friends aren't fighting. You feel happy. Life is just . . . good.

When you have one of those happy days, stop. Stop right where you are and thank God for it. Thank him for every single thing you can think of. Don't take anything for granted. And remember that feeling of gratefulness and joy. File it away in your heart somewhere so that the next time you're having a terrible, nothing-goes-right kind of day, you can remember the great

days and know that God is still working and
things will get better again soon.

CHECKUP TIME

On a scale of 1 to 5, what's your gratefulness level?

1 = never
2 = not very often
3 = sometimes
4 = most of the time
5 = always

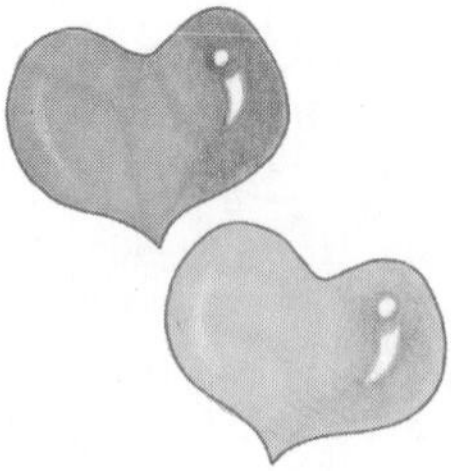

I thank God each day for the good things he does for me.

1   2   3   4   5

I remember God's care and faithfulness when I'm having a bad day.

1   2   3   4   5

I share my attitude of gratitude with others.

1   2   3   4   5

I look for the daily gifts God gives me.

1   2   3   4   5

People comment on the joy they see in me.

1   2   3   4   5

KEY

MOSTLY 1s Whoa! Dump the grump.

MOSTLY 2s You need to exercise your joy muscles.

MOSTLY 3s Right in the middle—not bad, but not great.

MOSTLY 4s There's some room for improvement.

MOSTLY 5s Happy, happy! Celebrate!

THINGS TO DO

☐ If you got mostly 1s and 2s on the quiz, it's time for an attitude adjustment. Choose one thing to thank God for right now.

☐ Make a list of all the good gifts God has given you.

☐ Write down a verse about praising God, such as Psalm 47:6 or Ephesians 5:20. Keep it with you for the hard times when you need a reminder.

☐ Write a note to someone and share your new attitude of joy with that person!

THINGS TO REMEMBER

I will be filled with joy because of you. I will sing praises to your name, O Most High. **PSALM 9:2**

Let the heavens be glad, and the earth rejoice! Let the sea and everything in it shout his praise! **PSALM 96:11**

Give thanks for everything to God the Father in the name of our Lord Jesus Christ. **EPHESIANS 5:20**

Always be full of joy in the Lord. I say it again—rejoice! **PHILIPPIANS 4:4**

You love him even though you have never seen him. Though you do not see him now, you trust him; and you rejoice with a glorious, inexpressible joy. **1 PETER 1:8**

Praising God is one of the highest and purest acts of religion. In prayer we act like men; in praise we act like angels.
THOMAS WATSON

God gave you a gift of 86,400 seconds today. Have you used one to say "thank you"?
WILLIAM A. WARD

Birds sing after a storm; why shouldn't people feel as free to delight in whatever remains to them?
ROSE KENNEDY

Home Alone

"I'M HOME," KELSEY called out. But even as she said it she knew there wouldn't be a response. No one was home. She and her mom lived alone, and Mom was still at work. Kelsey locked the door, then went through the apartment and turned on all the lights. She didn't like being alone, especially in the winter when it got dark so early.

Kelsey picked up the phone and dialed her mom's office. "I'm home," she said. That was their routine so Mom would know she was safe. Her mom's response was always pretty much the same: "Okay, get your homework done, honey. There are leftovers in the refrigerator for dinner. I'll be home before you go to bed."

Kelsey settled down at the kitchen table to do her homework . . . ugh, a history paper. *Mom would know how to do this stuff,* she thought. But Mom wouldn't be home for several hours, so Kelsey struggled through it, wondering if she was doing it right. When it was time for dinner she pulled out a slice of cold pizza and plopped it in the microwave. It wasn't that great, but she watched some TV while she ate it. All in all it was a pretty lonely afternoon and evening.

It might sound like fun sometimes to have no adults around. The rules that parents lay down can be pretty tough, and you might feel smothered by having them check up on you all the time. In some families, like Kelsey's, parents have to work late or there is only one parent at home. If that's the way your family is, you might come home from school to an empty home. That can get pretty lonely, can't it?

What do you do when you are alone and feeling lonely or maybe even a little scared? Is there an adult you can call if you're afraid? Can you talk things through with an older sibling or another relative? One thing you can do in any situation is talk to God. He knows when life is stinky and you feel alone. He cares.

CHECKUP TIME

On a scale of 1 to 5, how well do you handle being home alone?

1 = never
2 = not very often
3 = sometimes
4 = most of the time
5 = always

There are trusted people I can talk to when I'm home alone.

1   2   3   4   5

I follow the ground rules laid out for me when my parents aren't home.

1   2   3   4   5

I know what to do if a frightening situation comes up and my parents are gone.

1   2   3   4   5

I can talk through problems with my mom or dad.

1   2   3   4   5

I truly believe God is watching over me.

1   2   3   4   5

KEY

MOSTLY 1s Uh-oh. You don't feel good about being home alone at all.

MOSTLY 2s Anxiety is a problem for you, right?

MOSTLY 3s Average—sometimes you're okay by yourself, but sometimes you could use some courage.

MOSTLY 4s Most of the time you handle being alone pretty well.

MOSTLY 5s Good job! You know you are never truly alone.

THINGS TO DO

- ☐ Make a list of some things you and your parents can do to make you feel more comfortable about being home alone.
- ☐ Make a list of nearby neighbors or relatives you can call if you're frightened or lonely.
- ☐ Memorize Psalm 33:18. Say it over and over when you're afraid.
- ☐ Come up with a project to work on while you're home alone that will encourage someone else and keep you busy at the same time.

THINGS TO REMEMBER

The LORD watches over those who fear him, those who rely on his unfailing love. **PSALM 33:18**

I will be your God throughout your lifetime—until your hair is white with age. I made you, and I will care for you. I will carry you along and save you. **ISAIAH 46:4**

I have loved you, my people, with an everlasting love. With unfailing love I have drawn you to myself. **JEREMIAH 31:3**

The faithful love of the LORD never ends! His mercies never cease. **LAMENTATIONS 3:22**

If God cares so wonderfully for wildflowers that are here today and thrown into the fire tomorrow, he will certainly care for you. Why do you have so little faith? **MATTHEW 6:30**

> Only he who can say, "The Lord is the strength of my life" can say, "Of whom shall I be afraid?"
> ALEXANDER MACLAREN

> Of all the needs (there are none imaginary) a lonely child has, the one that must be satisfied, if there is going to be hope and a hope of wholeness, is the unshaken need for an unshakable God.
> MAYA ANGELOU

> Pray that your loneliness may spur you into finding something to live for.
> DAG HAMMARSKJÖLD

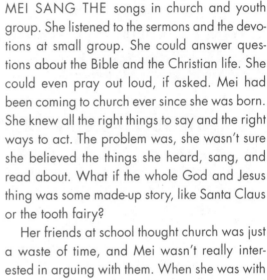

What If It's Not True?

MEI SANG THE songs in church and youth group. She listened to the sermons and the devotions at small group. She could answer questions about the Bible and the Christian life. She could even pray out loud, if asked. Mei had been coming to church ever since she was born. She knew all the right things to say and the right ways to act. The problem was, she wasn't sure she believed the things she heard, sang, and read about. What if the whole God and Jesus thing was some made-up story, like Santa Claus or the tooth fairy?

Her friends at school thought church was just a waste of time, and Mei wasn't really interested in arguing with them. When she was with them, thoughts about God hardly ever popped into her mind. When she was with her church friends, she knew exactly what to say and how to act to fit in with them. But truthfully, the reality of God hadn't moved into her heart. She had no personal relationship with him.

Mei's relationship with God was like a relationship she might have with the president. She knew who he was and respected him, but she didn't actually know him. Mei would never go to the president to talk over a problem or to ask his opinion about something. She didn't really know him. That's how she felt about God. She thought it was possible he might be real and mighty and powerful. But she thought all the stuff in the Bible didn't really have much to do with her.

When Mei's youth leader talked about God, he made it sound like God is a real person who cares about people's lives, like he actually loves and helps his people. *I'd like to know God like that,* she thought . . . but how?

Good question . . . how do you get from knowledge about God to a personal friendship with him? There are no shortcuts—the only answer is time. Spend time reading God's Word. Spend time talking to him and listening for his response. Time with God will build trust and confidence, and love will grow from that.

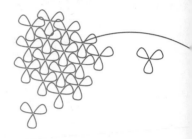

CHECKUP TIME

On a scale of 1 to 5, how is your belief level?

1 = never
2 = not very often
3 = sometimes
4 = most of the time
5 = always

I am intentional about growing in my relationship with God.
1   2   3   4   5

I believe God cares about what happens in my life.
1   2   3   4   5

I set aside time to talk to God.
1   2   3   4   5

I set aside time to read my Bible.
1   2   3   4   5

I act the same with my church friends and my school friends.
1   2   3   4   5

KEY

MOSTLY 1s God isn't a big part of your life, is he?

MOSTLY 2s Lukewarm is the best word for your faith.

MOSTLY 3s Well, it could be worse.

MOSTLY 4s You are starting to understand that God really loves you.

MOSTLY 5s Your relationship with God is real and personal. That's great!

THINGS TO DO

☐ Set a time every day to read God's Word.

☐ Pray honestly about whatever is going on in your life right now—God can take whatever you want to tell him.

☐ Next time the opportunity comes up, talk to someone about your faith, even if it's someone you don't usually talk to about spiritual things.

☐ Ask God to help you know him better and trust him more.

THINGS TO REMEMBER

Believe in the Lord Jesus and you will be saved. **ACTS 16:31**

God saved you by his grace when you believed. And you can't take credit for this; it is a gift from God. **EPHESIANS 2:8**

We are made right with God by placing our faith in Jesus Christ. And this is true for everyone who believes, no matter who we are. **ROMANS 3:22**

These are written so that you may continue to believe that Jesus is the Messiah, the Son of God, and that by believing in him you will have life by the power of his name. **JOHN 20:31**

It is impossible to please God without faith. Anyone who wants to come to him must believe that God exists and that he rewards those who sincerely seek him. **HEBREWS 11:6**

Faith is to believe what you do not yet see; the reward for this faith is to see what you believe.
AUGUSTINE

Only he who believes is obedient. Only he who is obedient believes.
DIETRICH BONHOEFFER

Take the first step in faith. You don't have to see the whole staircase, just take the first step.
MARTIN LUTHER KING JR.

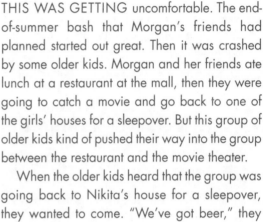

Standing Strong

> Don't let us yield to temptation, but rescue us from the evil one.
> MATTHEW 6:13

THIS WAS GETTING uncomfortable. The end-of-summer bash that Morgan's friends had planned started out great. Then it was crashed by some older kids. Morgan and her friends ate lunch at a restaurant at the mall, then they were going to catch a movie and go back to one of the girls' houses for a sleepover. But this group of older kids kind of pushed their way into the group between the restaurant and the movie theater.

When the older kids heard that the group was going back to Nikita's house for a sleepover, they wanted to come. "We've got beer," they offered. "We can bring it in under our coats. Your parents will never know." When Nikita said no thanks, they said, "Come on, grow up, will you? It will be fun!"

You may know some kids who drink because they think it makes them look cool. But they're wrong. Alcohol does harmful things to your brain, and on top of that, it can make you really sick to your stomach.

The temptation to drink in order to look cool really trips up some kids. They want to fit in, so they fall into the habit of drinking. But once you become a drinker, the only people you fit in with are the other drinkers. Alcohol messes up your brain—you can't think straight when you're in an alcohol fog. Then you end up doing things you wouldn't do if you were thinking straight.

God gave you one body and one brain. They

have to last you this entire life. Your body and brain are what you need to become successful, to have a career and a family. They need to be treated with respect. . . . Alcohol doesn't do that.

CHECKUP TIME

On a scale of 1 to 5, how do you do with temptation?

1 = never
2 = not very often
3 = sometimes
4 = most of the time
5 = always

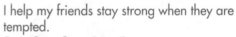

I stand up for what I know is right.
1   2   3   4   5

I care more about obeying God than what other people think.
1   2   3   4   5

I treat this body God has given me with respect.
1   2   3   4   5

I help my friends stay strong when they are tempted.
1   2   3   4   5

I have decided in advance what lines I refuse to cross.
1   2   3   4   5

KEY

MOSTLY 1s Uh-oh, temptation rules your life.

MOSTLY 2s You give in more often than not.

MOSTLY 3s Fifty-fifty: sometimes you're strong and sometimes you're not.

MOSTLY 4s There's room for improvement, but you're doing pretty well.

MOSTLY 5s Great! You trust God to be your strength!

THINGS TO DO

☐ Write a letter to God, confessing the areas where you
tend to give in to temptation. Commit to changing the
way you respond in those situations, and ask for his help.

☐ Make a deal with a friend to hold each other
accountable in resisting temptation.

☐ Come up with a backup plan you can put in place
next time you are in a tempting situation. Talk to your parents and
arrange for them or another trusted adult to pick you up at any time
of the day or night if you are getting pressured to drink or do drugs
or participate in something else you know is wrong.

☐ Memorize a verse that promises God's help and strength in your life,
such as Matthew 6:13 or Ephesians 6:11.

THINGS TO REMEMBER

I cling to you; your strong right hand holds
me securely. **PSALM 63:8**

Be on guard. Stand firm in the faith.
Be courageous. Be strong.
1 CORINTHIANS 16:13

Put on all of God's armor so that you will be able
to stand firm against all strategies of the devil.
EPHESIANS 6:11

These trials will show that your faith is genuine. It is
being tested as fire tests and purifies gold—though
your faith is far more precious than mere gold.
So when your faith remains strong through many
trials, it will bring you much praise and glory and
honor on the day when Jesus Christ is revealed to
the whole world. **1 PETER 1:7**

Stand firm against him, and be strong in your faith.
Remember that your Christian brothers and sisters
all over the world are going through the same kind
of suffering you are. **1 PETER 5:9**

*If you have been tempted
into evil, fly from it. It is
not falling into the water,
but lying in it, that drowns.*
UNKNOWN

*It is much easier to
suppress a first desire than
to satisfy those that follow.*
BENJAMIN FRANKLIN

*It is easier to stay out
than get out.*
MARK TWAIN

Gray Clouds

Let the Spirit renew your thoughts and attitudes.
EPHESIANS 4:23

JANIE PICKED UP her food tray and started for the table where all her friends were sitting. Of course, just as she passed a table full of guys, her plate slipped right off the tray. Luckily it didn't land on anyone's lap, but the gooey macaroni and cheese fell right at the feet of the guy Janie most wanted to notice her . . . but not like this!

It seemed like that was the story of her life right now. Nothing was going right. And because of that Janie had slipped into a major funk. She couldn't seem to find any joy in life anymore. Nothing was fun. Nothing was hopeful. Nothing brought her any satisfaction. She couldn't find any reason to be happy or look forward to the future. It was kind of scary.

If you've ever been there, you know how scary that place can be. Janie was depressed, and that can be serious. She was having trouble with her schoolwork. She didn't want to be with her friends. She couldn't get along with her parents. She didn't want to do anything except lie on her bed and stare at the ceiling. Everything seemed to take so much effort, and she just didn't have the energy to pull it off. It was easier to slip deeper into the emotional place where she just didn't care.

Depression can come on gradually, and sometimes you don't really notice it's happening. A lot of people struggle with depression at different levels. It doesn't mean they don't love God or aren't trying to live for him. In many cases, depression is an actual illness that requires professional help, just like a physical illness. In other situations, people can get depressed from having their priorities mixed up.

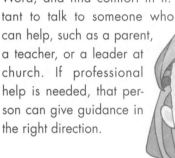

In Janie's case, she couldn't find anything to get excited about anymore. Every day seemed to begin with a gray cloud hanging over it—a cloud that never went away. So what could she do? A place to start is to talk to God, read his Word, and find comfort in it. It's also important to talk to someone who can help, such as a parent, a teacher, or a leader at church. If professional help is needed, that person can give guidance in the right direction.

CHECKUP TIME

On a scale of 1 to 5, how do you deal with depression?

1 = never
2 = not very often
3 = sometimes
4 = most of the time
5 = always

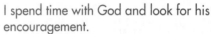

I talk to someone when life gets overwhelming.

1   2   3   4   5

There are bright spots in life that encourage me.

1   2   3   4   5

I choose to think about positive things instead of dwelling on negative thoughts.

1   2   3   4   5

I spend time with God and look for his encouragement.

1   2   3   4   5

I accept that there are good times and hard times in everyone's life.

1   2   3   4   5

KEY

MOSTLY 1s You'd better talk to someone and get some help.

MOSTLY 2s You're finding life hard to celebrate right now, aren't you?

MOSTLY 3s You're right in the middle—could be better and could be worse.

MOSTLY 4s You might feel down occasionally, but you have a healthy perspective on life.

MOSTLY 5s Great job! You're handling the difficult parts of life very well.

THINGS TO DO

☐ If you think you or one of your friends is struggling with depression, talk to someone you trust today to get some help.

☐ Make a list of all the great and wonderful things in your life.

☐ Make a list of all the things you have to look forward to—this week, this year, and for eternity. You have lots of reasons to have hope!

☐ Talk to God often about the things that make you sad or lonely. He cares what you're going through!

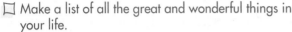

THINGS TO REMEMBER

Let your unfailing love surround us, LORD, for our hope is in you alone. **PSALM 33:22**

Why am I discouraged? Why is my heart so sad? I will put my hope in God! I will praise him again—my Savior and my God! **PSALM 42:5-6**

"I know the plans I have for you," says the LORD. "They are plans for good and not for disaster, to give you a future and a hope." **JEREMIAH 29:11**

We can rejoice, too, when we run into problems and trials, for we know that they help us develop endurance. And endurance develops strength of character, and character strengthens our confident hope of salvation. **ROMANS 5:3-4**

I pray that your hearts will be flooded with light so that you can understand the confident hope he has given to those he called—his holy people who are his rich and glorious inheritance. **EPHESIANS 1:18**

Depression is a prison where you are both the suffering prisoner and the cruel jailer.
DOROTHY ROWE

*"It's snowing still," said Eeyore gloomily.
"So it is."
"And freezing."
"Is it?"
"Yes," said Eeyore.
"However," he said, brightening up a little, "we haven't had an earthquake lately."*
A. A. MILNE, FROM THE HOUSE AT POOH CORNER

Everyone thinks his own burden heavy.
FRENCH PROVERB

Double Negative

Kind words are like honey—sweet to the soul and healthy for the body.
PROVERBS 16:24

"THIS HOT LUNCH is nasty, as usual. It tastes like they cooked it three days ago," Dana complained. Aisha quietly stepped back. She didn't want to be in the line of fire for Dana's criticisms. It had happened before: "Why do you talk to Patricia? She's weird—you don't want to be her friend." "Your hair looks like you haven't washed it for three weeks." "Cool outfit, Aisha—did you get it at a resale shop?" Dana's criticisms could be brutal. The thing was, nothing was ever good enough for Dana. She could find something negative in any situation, and she wasn't afraid to point it out to others.

Wow, it's no fun to be around someone like Dana, is it? When you're with someone who is constantly critical, it's easy for that negative spirit to rub off on you. Before you know it, you find yourself complaining about stuff too. A person who is always negative is not a happy person. There are probably some things she doesn't like about herself. She can't or won't deal with those things head-on, but her feelings come out in her criticism of everything and everyone else!

Are you one of those people? Stop and think about the last five comments you made. Were they criticizing someone or something? Can you think of the last honest compliment you gave someone? If you are more often critical than kind, do you know why? Are you unhappy deep inside? Or perhaps you feel like life owes you something—more happiness or more stuff—and being crabby about that comes out in a bad attitude. Whatever is going on inside you, it's better to deal with it and get past it, for your sake and everyone else's. Then you can look for the positive things around you and become a kinder, gentler person.

Did you know that your attitude makes a difference to God? Yep, God's Word encourages you to be thankful and joyful in all that God gives you. Does that mean you'll never be unhappy? Of course not, but don't dwell on it. Look for the good in your situations and in the people around you. Remember that loving others (not criticizing them) is God's command to you!

CHECKUP TIME

On a scale of 1 to 5, how critical are you?

1 = never
2 = not very often
3 = sometimes
4 = most of the time
5 = always

I look for the positive in a situation.
1   2   3   4   5

My friends say I'm fun to be with.
1   2   3   4   5

Deep down, I am happy with my life.
1   2   3   4   5

I try to spend time with people who have positive attitudes.
1   2   3   4   5

I control what I say and offer compliments instead of criticisms.
1   2   3   4   5

KEY

MOSTLY 1s You are so negative, there might as well be a minus sign above your head!

MOSTLY 2s Based on your critical attitude, you must not like yourself very much.

MOSTLY 3s Right in the middle—could be better and could be worse.

MOSTLY 4s You do pretty well at staying positive.

MOSTLY 5s Great! You've got control of your attitude.

THINGS TO DO

- ☐ Next time you find yourself around someone who is complaining, make an effort to say something uplifting in response.
- ☐ Each day, say one positive thing—out loud—to someone.
- ☐ Give an honest compliment to someone this week.
- ☐ Ask God to help you stop being critical.

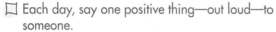

THINGS TO REMEMBER

An angry person starts fights; a hot-tempered person commits all kinds of sin.
PROVERBS 29:22

Don't you see how wonderfully kind, tolerant, and patient God is with you? Does this mean nothing to you? Can't you see that his kindness is intended to turn you from your sin?
ROMANS 2:4

If you have a gift for showing kindness to others, do it gladly. **ROMANS 12:8**

Do everything without complaining and arguing, so that no one can criticize you. **PHILIPPIANS 2:14-15**

The Holy Spirit produces this kind of fruit in our lives: love, joy, peace, patience, kindness, goodness, faithfulness, gentleness, and self-control. There is no law against these things!
GALATIANS 5:22-23

If you scatter thorns, don't go barefoot.
ITALIAN PROVERB

Those who bring sunshine into the lives of others cannot keep it from themselves.
JAMES M. BARRIE

To speak ill of others is a dishonest way of praising ourselves.
WILL DURANT

I'm Bored!

"THERE'S NOTHING to do!" Ellie whined. She kicked a sofa pillow into the air. It slammed against a lamp, which teetered and tottered before falling from the table. Thankfully the lamp didn't break, but the whole scene was the last straw for Ellie's mom.

"If you're bored, I can certainly give you a few suggestions for things to do," she offered.

"Like what?" Ellie asked. She didn't think she would like Mom's ideas.

"You could clean up your room. It looks like a tornado blew through it," Mom suggested.

"That's even more boring than doing nothing," Ellie whined again.

"Why don't you write thank-you notes for your birthday gifts? Those notes are about a month overdue already," Mom said.

"I'm not in the mood for that right now," Ellie said as she kicked another pillow into the air.

Mom caught the pillow and said, "Ellie, get off the couch right now. It's not my job to keep you entertained. There are plenty of things you could do—visit a neighbor, call your grandmother, walk the dog, bake cookies, or even read a book. You just don't want to do anything that sounds like work."

Whoa, sounds like Mom had finally had it, huh? Yeah, when parents see their kids being self-centered or lazy, it doesn't take long for their patience to run out.

Do you ever get bored? Almost all of us do at some point. But when you think about it, there is never a time when you have absolutely, positively nothing to do. There are just things that you may not *want* to do. Well, that's okay. Everyone has preferences. But rather than getting destructive around the house or whining to your parents, are you willing to do something that is productive and a good use of your time? Even if it sounds like work?

Guess what? When you're willing to use your time in a useful way by serving others or helping around the house or just doing things that are expected of you . . . well, that's a sign of maturity! Remember that God gives you twenty-four hours each day. Some of those hours are spent sleeping, some are spent having fun, and some are spent doing work. Make an effort to use your hours wisely so that God is honored by your life!

CHECKUP TIME

On a scale of 1 to 5, how are you doing with handling boredom?

1 = never
2 = not very often
3 = sometimes
4 = most of the time
5 = always

I do what my parents expect of me without being asked.
1   2   3   4   5

When I'm bored, I can find things to do.
1   2   3   4   5

I'm willing to do things that sound like work.
1   2   3   4   5

I spend my time doing useful, productive things.
1   2   3   4   5

I believe God has a purpose for how I spend my time.
1   2   3   4   5

KEY

MOSTLY 1s Whoa, you'd better read this devo again and take an honest look at how you spend your time.

MOSTLY 2s You've got some work to do. . . . Sorry to say that word!

MOSTLY 3s Okay, you don't completely depend on others to keep you entertained, but there is certainly room for improvement.

MOSTLY 4s You're doing well, but there's room to grow.

MOSTLY 5s You're showing some real maturity. Great job!

THINGS TO DO

- ☐ Make a list of things to do—anything you can think of, from work stuff to fun stuff. Keep it in your room to refer to the next time you get bored.
- ☐ Make a second list of people you know who could use some encouragement, and then list things you could do to help them.
- ☐ Make a third list that records how you spend your time for one week. At the end of the week, look at how much time you spend watching TV, talking on the phone, or being on the computer. Are there some areas where you could be wiser about how you spend your time?
- ☐ Write down a verse about how to spend your time, such as Ephesians 5:16 or Colossians 3:23, and tape it to your computer or phone or wherever you are tempted to waste time.

THINGS TO REMEMBER

Lazy people take food in their hand but don't even lift it to their mouth.
PROVERBS 26:15

Make the most of every opportunity in these evil days. **EPHESIANS 5:16**

Stay away from all believers who live idle lives and don't follow the tradition they received from us. For you know that you ought to imitate us. We were not idle when we were with you. . . . Even while we were with you, we gave you this command: "Those unwilling to work will not get to eat."
2 THESSALONIANS 3:6-7, 10

To those who use well what they are given, even more will be given, and they will have an abundance. But from those who do nothing, even what little they have will be taken away. **MATTHEW 25:29**

Work willingly at whatever you do, as though you were working for the Lord rather than for people.
COLOSSIANS 3:23

Watch your thoughts, for they become words. Watch your words, for they become actions. Watch your actions, for they become habits. Watch your habits, for they become character. Watch your character, for it becomes your destiny.
UNKNOWN

Laziness is nothing more than the habit of resting before you get tired.
JULES RENARD

In the long run, we shape our lives, and we shape ourselves. . . . The choices we make are ultimately our own responsibility.
ELEANOR ROOSEVELT

How Do You Heal a Broken Heart?

HURT. SAD. EMBARRASSED. Scared. Sad again. So sad. Those were some of the things Destiny had felt in the past few hours. But no words could actually capture the pain in her heart. The person Destiny looked up to the most was her mom's brother, Uncle Gary. He was the main adult male in her world since her dad had left. Uncle Gary could make her laugh. He had taught her how to play softball. They went on Gary-Destiny dates for ice cream sundaes. She could talk to him about anything. He was awesome.

But Destiny's mom had just told her that Uncle Gary was arrested for buying drugs from an undercover cop. *Uncle Gary does drugs?* Destiny couldn't get her brain to wrap around that.

"It has to be a mistake. Uncle Gary wouldn't do that," Destiny protested. Her mom just sighed and said that he would have to go to jail.

Destiny's friends knew how much Uncle Gary meant to her. What would they think when they found out about this? What would they say to her? Destiny wanted to scream, but all she could do was cry. She felt terrible every time she thought about her uncle in jail. Destiny thought her heart would never stop hurting.

When your heart is aching, everything in life seems to have a cloud over it. You can't think of anything that will make you feel better except fixing whatever broke your heart in the first place.

And most of the time you have no control over that. So what do you do? How do you keep going when your heart is hurting so much?

There is no simple answer to that question, but you can start by trusting God and praying for his strength and help. Although it may take a while, you'll eventually get to the place where you truly trust in God and you know that your prayers make a difference. In the meantime, you'll still hurt, and that's okay. Tell God how you feel—he can take it if you're frustrated or even angry with him. He understands if you're confused and scared. Tell him. You'll feel better, and it will move you closer to the place of trusting him so he can heal your broken heart.

CHECKUP TIME

On a scale of 1 to 5, how do you handle things when your heart is hurting?

1 = never
2 = not very often
3 = sometimes
4 = most of the time
5 = always

When I'm hurting, I talk to someone about my feelings instead of withdrawing from people.
1   2   3   4   5

I am honest with God about how I'm feeling.
1   2   3   4   5

I believe my prayers make a difference.
1   2   3   4   5

Deep down, I trust God to take care of things.
1   2   3   4   5

I comfort people when they are going through tough times.
1   2   3   4   5

KEY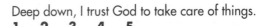

MOSTLY 1s Uh-oh, you're in some serious pain. Find someone trustworthy to talk with . . . now!

MOSTLY 2s Well, let's be honest: you still need some help dealing with your hurt.

MOSTLY 3s Sometimes you feel pretty heartbroken, but you're doing okay.

MOSTLY 4s You have a pretty good idea how to cope when you're hurting.

MOSTLY 5s Good job. You know how to handle pain well.

THINGS TO DO

- ☐ Think about a godly adult you trust. Ask if you can talk with her when you are dealing with a difficult issue.

- ☐ Memorize some verses about how much God loves you, such as Psalm 56:8 or Isaiah 49:13. Write them down and put them in places where you see them every day.

- ☐ Pray. Pray. Pray. It does help.

- ☐ Cry. Yeah, go ahead and cry. It's good to get those emotions out, and it helps you feel better.

THINGS TO REMEMBER

You keep track of all my sorrows. You have collected all my tears in your bottle. You have recorded each one in your book.
PSALM 56:8

Show me your unfailing love in wonderful ways. By your mighty power you rescue those who seek refuge from their enemies. **PSALM 17:7**

The LORD has comforted his people and will have compassion on them in their suffering. **ISAIAH 49:13**

We fasted and earnestly prayed that our God would take care of us, and he heard our prayer. **EZRA 8:23**

Weeping may last through the night, but joy comes with the morning. **PSALM 30:5**

Pain is never permanent.
SAINT TERESA

Perhaps our eyes need to be washed by our tears once in a while, so that we can see Life with a clearer view again.
ALEX TAN

I know God will not give me anything I can't handle. I just wish He didn't trust me so much.
MOTHER TERESA

Did You Hear . . . ?

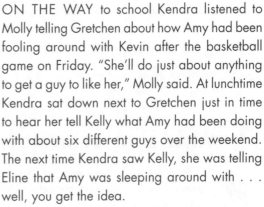

Jesus replied, "'You must love the LORD your God with all your heart, all your soul, and all your mind.' This is the first and greatest commandment. A second is equally important: 'Love your neighbor as yourself.'"
MATTHEW 22:37-39

ON THE WAY to school Kendra listened to Molly telling Gretchen about how Amy had been fooling around with Kevin after the basketball game on Friday. "She'll do just about anything to get a guy to like her," Molly said. At lunchtime Kendra sat down next to Gretchen just in time to hear her tell Kelly what Amy had been doing with about six different guys over the weekend. The next time Kendra saw Kelly, she was telling Eline that Amy was sleeping around with . . . well, you get the idea.

Gossip. It just grows and grows until it takes on a life of its own. One little bit of information (whether it's true or not) can grow into a massive story that totally wrecks a person's reputation. It doesn't really matter if the information is a little true or completely false. In this case, Kendra didn't know if the part about Amy and Kevin even happened, and then the story got stretched way beyond that. Not fair—to Amy or to the people hearing the gossip.

Spreading gossip about another person is just plain old mean. But the thing you might not have thought about is that there's often a subconscious desire on the part of the gossiper to make herself feel more important than the person she's talking about. Whew, that can get dangerous. It can backfire when the truth comes out and the gossiper ends up looking like a fool . . . a mean fool. And in the long run, gossiping about someone else makes you feel *worse* about yourself, not better.

The thing is that God made it a point (several times) to tell us to love each other. He said to love others the way you love yourself. And you wouldn't spread rumors about yourself, would you? It's a pretty good guess that loving someone means saying kind things about her, not gossiping about her. Put on the brakes when it comes to gossip, because it matters how you treat others—God said so.

CHECKUP TIME

On a scale of 1 to 5, how are you doing at controlling gossip?

1 = never
2 = not very often
3 = sometimes
4 = most of the time
5 = always

When I hear some gossip—no matter how juicy it is—I let it go in one ear and out the other.
1   2   3   4   5

I want others to be successful and well liked.
1   2   3   4   5

I control the urge to share "news" about others.
1   2   3   4   5

If I hear people saying something mean behind someone's back, I find something nice to say about the person.
1   2   3   4   5

If my friends start gossiping, I try to change the course of the conversation.
1   2   3   4   5

KEY

MOSTLY 1s Oh wow. You must be the gossip queen. Make a decision now to stop the gossip train!

MOSTLY 2s Well, it looks like you need some help. Choose one area from this quiz and start working on it.

MOSTLY 3s You could be a much better friend to others.

MOSTLY 4s Not bad, but there's room for improvement.

MOSTLY 5s Good job. You are definitely showing love to others.

THINGS TO DO

- ☐ Make a commitment to say only kind things behind people's backs. Put it in writing, and sign your name to it.

- ☐ Make an agreement with your friends to put the brakes on gossip.

- ☐ Apologize to one person who has been hurt by gossip that you and your friends have had a part in sharing.

- ☐ Ask God to help you avoid spreading gossip and show true kindness to others.

THINGS TO REMEMBER

We all make many mistakes. For if we could control our tongues, we would be perfect and could also control ourselves in every other way. **JAMES 3:2**

Don't use foul or abusive language. Let everything you say be good and helpful, so that your words will be an encouragement to those who hear them. **EPHESIANS 4:29**

I am giving you a new commandment: Love each other. Just as I have loved you, you should love each other. **JOHN 13:34**

A troublemaker plants seeds of strife; gossip separates the best of friends. **PROVERBS 16:28**

We love each other because he loved us first.
1 JOHN 4:19

Who gossips with you will gossip of you.
IRISH QUOTE

Gossip needn't be false to be evil—there's a lot of truth that shouldn't be passed around.
FRANK A. CLARK

To love another person is to see the face of God.
FROM LES MISÉRABLES

Do the Crime, Do the Time

"KYLIE, I SAID I'm sorry like a hundred times. What else can I do? Come on, call me back." Kylie listened to the message from her best friend (well, former best friend). In fact, she listened to it over and over . . . then deleted it. She was not going to call Maggie back.

She and Maggie had been best friends since first grade. They were always together—they liked the same things, laughed at inside jokes, and finished each other's sentences. Kylie had trusted Maggie completely. Then one day Kylie heard another friend blabbing one of her secrets. Kylie hadn't told anyone except Maggie. So Kylie immediately shut Maggie out of her life, and no matter how much Maggie apologized and begged for forgiveness, Kylie refused to even talk to her.

In Kylie's mind, it made perfect sense—Maggie had broken her trust, and she would not get a second chance. Kylie wasn't big on forgiveness . . . unless she was the one who needed forgiving. She didn't seem to make the connection that she made mistakes and needed her friends to forgive her, and that her friends made mistakes and needed her forgiveness too. The thing about Kylie (and pretty much anyone who is unwilling to forgive others) is that everything is all about *her*.

Let's be honest: some things are easier to forgive than others. When you are faced with one of those hurts that is hard to get over—you know, when it feels like someone has kicked you in the stomach and you can't even catch your breath— that's when you need supernatural power to be able to forgive. Assuming you aren't a superhero, where will that power come from?

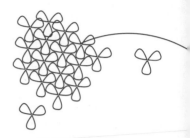

Fortunately we don't have to dig up that kind of power from somewhere inside ourselves; it comes from God. Remember that God commands you to love others. Well, you can't love and hold a grudge at the same time. So to be obedient to God, you definitely need his strength to forgive those who have hurt you. Through his grace, you can offer them a second, third, or fourth chance . . . or however many they need. It's not easy (no kidding), but you'll be glad you did it.

CHECKUP TIME

On a scale of 1 to 5, how are you at forgiving?

1 = never
2 = not very often
3 = sometimes
4 = most of the time
5 = always

I willingly give my friends another chance when they hurt me.

1 2 3 4 5

I give people the opportunity to apologize and explain their actions.

1 2 3 4 5

I forgive others, even when it is hard.

1 2 3 4 5

I ask others to forgive me when I hurt them.

1 2 3 4 5

I ask God to help me when it's difficult to forgive.

1 2 3 4 5

KEY

MOSTLY 1s Wow, at this rate, you're going to be lonely soon!

MOSTLY 2s You need some help. Choose one area from this quiz and start working on it.

MOSTLY 3s Middle of the road isn't good enough. Ask God to help you with this forgiveness thing.

MOSTLY 4s There's still room for improvement.

MOSTLY 5s Excellent. You have a wonderful forgiving spirit.

THINGS TO DO

☐ Is there anyone who is no longer in your life because you wouldn't forgive him or her? Try to contact that person and make a step toward healing the relationship.

☐ Make a list of the times your friends have forgiven you and given you a second chance.

☐ Confess to God any times you've been selfish and refused to forgive others.

☐ Memorize a verse about forgiveness, such as Proverbs 17:9 or Luke 17:4. Say it out loud every day.

THINGS TO REMEMBER

Love prospers when a fault is forgiven, but dwelling on it separates close friends. **PROVERBS 17:9**

Forgive us our sins, as we have forgiven those who sin against us. **MATTHEW 6:12**

If you forgive those who sin against you, your heavenly Father will forgive you. But if you refuse to forgive others, your Father will not forgive your sins. **MATTHEW 6:14-15**

When you are praying, first forgive anyone you are holding a grudge against, so that your Father in heaven will forgive your sins, too. **MARK 11:25**

Even if that person wrongs you seven times a day and each time turns again and asks forgiveness, you must forgive. **LUKE 17:4**

To forgive is to set a prisoner free and discover that the prisoner was you.
LEWIS B. SMEDES

He who cannot forgive others breaks the bridge over which he himself must pass.
GEORGE HERBERT

He who is devoid of the power to forgive is devoid of the power of love.
MARTIN LUTHER KING JR.

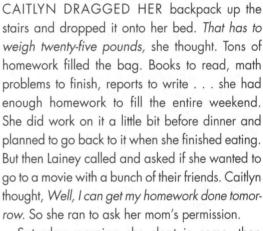

Never Put Off till Tomorrow . . .

CAITLYN DRAGGED HER backpack up the stairs and dropped it onto her bed. *That has to weigh twenty-five pounds,* she thought. Tons of homework filled the bag. Books to read, math problems to finish, reports to write . . . she had enough homework to fill the entire weekend. She did work on it a little bit before dinner and planned to go back to it when she finished eating. But then Lainey called and asked if she wanted to go to a movie with a bunch of their friends. Caitlyn thought, *Well, I can get my homework done tomorrow.* So she ran to ask her mom's permission.

Saturday morning she slept in some, then planned to get right on her homework. But Sophie stopped by and they got busy talking and doing their nails, and before Caitlyn knew it, Mom was calling her to dinner. They had company for dinner, and it would have been rude for Caitlyn to disappear. The two little girls who were visiting would have hunted her down anyway. Sunday morning, of course, was church. After lunch Caitlyn headed to her room to attack the bag of homework. But she checked her computer first and saw that a bunch of friends were online. Suddenly it was 10:00 and barely any of her homework was done. Caitlyn had managed to procrastinate the whole weekend away.

Isn't it funny that we rarely procrastinate when we're doing things we enjoy doing? How often do you tell your friends that you really can't talk right now or you can't hang out over the weekend? Yeah, probably not that often. Procrastination usually happens when you have to do things like homework or chores—things you do alone that are your responsibilities at home or for school.

There is always a price to pay when you put off doing things you need to do. People count on you to fulfill your responsibilities. When you don't do those things, you let others down and usually pay the consequences. People will begin to think they can't depend on you. The best plan is to work first and play later. Fulfill your responsibilities, then enjoy life.

Strange as it may sound, God's Word actually says something about homework. We're told in Colossians 3:23 and Proverbs 12:11 to work hard because that brings glory to God. So make an effort to do everything—including schoolwork—in a way that brings God glory.

CHECKUP TIME

On a scale of 1 to 5, where are you on the procrastination scale?

1 = never
2 = not very often
3 = sometimes
4 = most of the time
5 = always

I do my homework or chores before spending time with my friends.

1   2   3   4   5

It's important to me that others can depend on me.

1   2   3   4   5

I am responsible with my choices and how I spend my time.

1   2   3   4   5

I meet the deadlines my teachers and parents give me.

1   2   3   4   5

I do my best, whatever I'm working on.

1   2   3   4   5

KEY

MOSTLY 1s Eek, do you ever get anything done?

MOSTLY 2s You need some help. Choose one area from this quiz and start working on it.

MOSTLY 3s Middle of the road isn't good enough. Ask God to help you manage your time better.

MOSTLY 4s You usually get things done on time.

MOSTLY 5s Excellent! You manage your time well.

THINGS TO DO

☐ Make a list of your responsibilities. Prioritize your list as to what needs to be done first.

☐ Keep a notebook of how you spend your time for one week. Then look over it at the end of the week and decide how you can use your time more wisely.

☐ Ask a friend to hold you accountable for things you need to get done.

☐ Set aside a specific time and place to do your homework each day. Make sure there's nothing to distract you there, such as a TV, a phone, or music.

THINGS TO REMEMBER

Take a lesson from the ants, you lazybones. Learn from their ways and become wise! **PROVERBS 6:6**

A little extra sleep, a little more slumber, a little folding of the hands to rest—then poverty will pounce on you like a bandit.
PROVERBS 6:10-11

Those who live only to satisfy their own sinful nature will harvest decay and death from that sinful nature. But those who live to please the Spirit will harvest everlasting life from the Spirit.
GALATIANS 6:8

Good planning and hard work lead to prosperity, but hasty shortcuts lead to poverty. **PROVERBS 21:5**

Lazy people want much but get little, but those who work hard will prosper. **PROVERBS 13:4**

Leave nothing for tomorrow which can be done today.
ABRAHAM LINCOLN

The hardest work in the world is that which should have been done yesterday.
UNKNOWN

While we are postponing, life speeds by.
SENECA

A Big Red S

ISABELLA WALKED DOWN the hall of her school with her head bowed low. She kind of hugged the wall as she walked. She didn't make eye contact with anyone. She went to class and then straight home. She didn't laugh with her friends anymore—in fact, she barely even talked to them when they came up to her at school or called her on the phone. At home she stayed in her room except when she had to come out for meals.

Everyone knows what I did, she thought. It seemed to her that there was a big red *S* tattooed on her forehead announcing her sin to the world. *If I could just go back in time, I'd never have done it. It wasn't worth it at all.* But of course, she didn't have access to a time machine, so she couldn't change what she had done. Isabella was in agony over her actions, even though no one else knew. Sure, it had felt good at the time, but she knew what she'd done was wrong, even if it was a secret from everyone else.

Isabella didn't get caught, but she still felt like everyone knew what she'd done. That's called guilt. Isabella had known that what she was doing was wrong, but she'd done it anyway. And now she was living with guilt. When you feel guilty, it does seem as though you have a big red *S* on your forehead—like everyone must know what you did. Your conscience is nagging you to set things straight, and it's making you so miserable, you'll never want to do that wrong thing again.

Listen to your conscience. Guilt affects your whole life. Your friendships are bothered because you are hiding something from the people close to you and it strains your relationship. Your family life is affected because your guilt makes you short tempered and crabby. And your connection with God is affected too. Adam and Eve hid from God after they sinned because they felt guilty. Well, you probably try to hide from him in some way too when you have knowingly sinned and feel guilty about it. The best solution to guilt is . . . don't do things that make you feel guilty! But when you do, you can tell God about it and ask his forgiveness. He will forgive you and take away the guilt! He loves you that much.

CHECKUP TIME

On a scale of 1 to 5, what's your guilt level?

1 = never
2 = not very often
3 = sometimes
4 = most of the time
5 = always

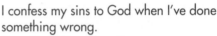

I do the right thing, even when it's hard.
1   2   3   4   5

I know wrong is wrong, even if I don't get caught.
1   2   3   4   5

I listen to my conscience.
1   2   3   4   5

I confess my sins to God when I've done something wrong.
1   2   3   4   5

When I've hurt someone, I do whatever I can to make things right with that person again.
1   2   3   4   5

KEY

MOSTLY 1s Your conscience needs some serious attention.

MOSTLY 2s You have some work to do. Choose one area from this quiz and start working on it.

MOSTLY 3s This is one of those times when average won't do.

MOSTLY 4s You deal with sin pretty honestly—but you can do better.

MOSTLY 5s Good job. Honesty keeps guilt away from you!

THINGS TO DO

☐ Confess anything you've done that is causing you guilt right now, and ask God for forgiveness. If you've hurt someone else by your actions, ask that person for forgiveness too.

☐ Write down things you feel guilty about on separate pieces of paper. One by one, thank God that his grace covers each thing, and then shred the papers into tiny pieces as a symbol of God's forgiveness.

☐ Think about some of the patterns in your life that cause you to feel guilty. Find a friend who will keep you accountable in those particular areas.

☐ Ask for God's help with future choices.

THINGS TO REMEMBER

Keep your servant from deliberate sins! Don't let them control me. Then I will be free of guilt and innocent of great sin. **PSALM 19:13**

The LORD is slow to get angry, but his power is great, and he never lets the guilty go unpunished. He displays his power in the whirlwind and the storm. The billowing clouds are the dust beneath his feet. **NAHUM 1:3**

The person who keeps all of the laws except one is as guilty as a person who has broken all of God's laws. **JAMES 2:10**

Remember, it is sin to know what you ought to do and then not do it. **JAMES 4:17**

You forgave the guilt of your people—yes, you covered all their sins. **PSALM 85:2**

Conscience is the root of all true courage; if a man would be brave let him obey his conscience.
JAMES FREEMAN CLARKE

I have come to the conclusion that none of us in our generation feels as guilty about sin as we should or as our forefathers did.
FRANCIS SCHAEFFER

The guilty think all talk is of themselves.
GEOFFREY CHAUCER

I Give Up

"I CAN'T DO IT! I give up!" Linnie threw her math book across the kitchen in complete frustration.

Her mom peeked her head in the kitchen when she heard the book hit the floor. "What's going on?" she asked. One look at Linnie's tearstained face and the math book on the floor answered the question. Linnie's mom picked up the book and laid it on the table. "Can I try to help you with your homework?"

"No. I give up. I'm too dumb to do this kind of math," Linnie said heatedly. "I've tried and tried, and I can't do it. It doesn't make any sense to me. I'm not trying anymore!"

Any person who is math challenged can understand Linnie's frustration. But is giving up the best answer? It may be the easiest answer in the short term, but it isn't the best one. When you're faced with a difficult challenge, you might wish you could just ignore it and hope it goes away, but that doesn't really solve the core of the problem, does it?

So what other options might Linnie have? One idea would be to accept her mom's help. Another would be to ask her teacher for extra help outside of class or find a friend to study with. She also might want to consider how well she has paid attention in class and applied herself to learning the material. The point is, there are almost always options other than giving up when something is difficult.

Quitting means you will never learn the lesson you're struggling with and you'll never have success at the task. It will always be unfinished business in your past. A better option is to look for ways to tackle what's in front of you. Then you'll have the satisfaction of finishing the job, learning a lesson or two, and moving on to the next challenge.

God's plan for your life isn't for it to be a failure. He truly wants you to succeed. So don't quit when things get tough. Instead, keep trying your best and look for the people he has placed around you to be helpers and mentors.

CHECKUP TIME

On a scale of 1 to 5, what's your attitude about giving up?

1 = never
2 = not very often
3 = sometimes
4 = most of the time
5 = always

When the going gets tough, I just work harder.
1   2   3   4   5

I ask for help when I need it.
1   2   3   4   5

I like to learn new things, even if they're challenging.
1   2   3   4   5

I finish the things I start.
1   2   3   4   5

I'd rather struggle than give up.
1   2   3   4   5

KEY

MOSTLY 1s It's time to set some goals for yourself!

MOSTLY 2s Choose one thing to work on—and don't give up.

MOSTLY 3s You are only a quitter half the time. You can do better.

MOSTLY 4s Not bad, but there's some room for improvement.

MOSTLY 5s Good job. You are a hard worker who is persistent!

THINGS TO DO

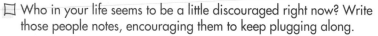

- ☐ Think of an area in your life where you are often tempted to give up. Make a list of what your options are besides giving up.

- ☐ Ask a friend or a mentor to be your cheerleader. Whenever you are faced with a difficult challenge, encourage each other to finish strong.

- ☐ Who in your life seems to be a little discouraged right now? Write those people notes, encouraging them to keep plugging along.

- ☐ Ask God to help you be persistent and work through the hard times.

THINGS TO REMEMBER

I am certain that God, who began the good work within you, will continue his work until it is finally finished on the day when Christ Jesus returns. **PHILIPPIANS 1:6**

Let's not get tired of doing what is good. At just the right time we will reap a harvest of blessing if we don't give up. **GALATIANS 6:9**

Keep on asking, and you will receive what you ask for. Keep on seeking, and you will find. Keep on knocking, and the door will be opened to you. **MATTHEW 7:7**

The LORD helps the fallen and lifts those bent beneath their loads. **PSALM 145:14**

He gives power to the weak and strength to the powerless. **ISAIAH 40:29**

Never, never—in nothing great or small, large or petty—never give in except to convictions of honor and good sense. WINSTON CHURCHILL

Consider the postage stamp. . . . It secures success through its ability to stick to one thing till it gets there. JOSH BILLINGS

We can do anything we want to if we stick to it long enough. HELEN KELLER

The Courtroom of Your Heart

BECKY WAS NEW to Middleton. Her family had moved about halfway through the school year. Coming into a new school was hard enough, but it was even worse when the semester had already begun. The groups of friends were already together, and no one really wanted to bother with the new girl. What made it worse was that some of her classmates had formed opinions of her without even getting to know her.

She'd been there only a week, and already she'd heard things like, "Did you see what that new girl wears? Is she from Mars or something?" or "Wow, how did that new girl make it this far in school? She reads like a first grader." Some kids made fun of what she brought for lunch. Others laughed at her accent. Becky felt like she had been put on trial and judged unworthy of being a part of this school—all without her being able to say a word to defend herself.

Judging others happens so easily. There's a "herd mentality" to it, where everyone who belongs to a certain group judges those who are on the outside. When you judge other people, they pretty much always come up short. It's not fair, but it happens. Before you judge someone else, take a moment to consider how it would feel to be on the other side of that experience. Being judged unworthy by others is not fun, especially when you don't get a fair trial.

There's another element to consider about judging others—it's a sin. No kidding. God said to take care of the problems in your own life before you start pointing out the issues in someone else's life. The things you judge as being wrong with other people may be the very things that will be judged wrong with you. God also said we need to love one another. It's a scientific fact that two elements cannot occupy the same space at the same time. That means a spirit of love and a spirit of judgment cannot both live in your heart. It's your choice: do you want to be someone who loves others, like God calls us to do, or someone who judges others in disobedience?

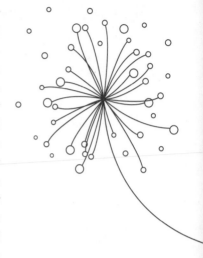

CHECKUP TIME

On a scale of 1 to 5, how judgmental are you?

1 = never
2 = not very often
3 = sometimes
4 = most of the time
5 = always

When I meet someone new, I get to know her before forming an opinion of her.
1   2   3   4   5

I try to slow my friends down when they start judging someone.
1   2   3   4   5

I take care of my own problems instead of criticizing others.
1   2   3   4   5

I like to make new friends, especially with people who are different from me.
1   2   3   4   5

It's important to me to show God's love to others.
1   2   3   4   5

KEY

MOSTLY 1s Choose one statement above to begin working on in your life.

MOSTLY 2s You have some work to do to become more accepting of others.

MOSTLY 3s So-so. You can do better.

MOSTLY 4s Not bad, but there's some room for improvement.

MOSTLY 5s Good job. You are a good reflection of God's love!

THINGS TO DO

☐ Make a list of people at school, at church, or in your neighborhood you could get to know—especially those who are different from you.

☐ Get together with your friends and make a commitment to cut the judging and start the loving.

☐ Apologize to anyone you may have unfairly judged in the past.

☐ Look at your own life and see what changes need to be made. Ask for God's forgiveness, and then pray for his help to make those changes.

THINGS TO REMEMBER

Do not judge others, and you will not be judged. Do not condemn others, or it will all come back against you. Forgive others, and you will be forgiven.
LUKE 6:37

You will be treated as you treat others. The standard you use in judging is the standard by which you will be judged. And why worry about a speck in your friend's eye when you have a log in your own? **MATTHEW 7:2-3**

Since you judge others for doing these things, why do you think you can avoid God's judgment when you do the same things? **ROMANS 2:3**

If anyone claims, "I am living in the light," but hates a Christian brother or sister, that person is still living in darkness. **1 JOHN 2:9**

God alone, who gave the law, is the Judge. He alone has the power to save or to destroy. So what right do you have to judge your neighbor?
JAMES 4:12

If you judge people, you have no time to love them.
MOTHER TERESA

Criticizing others is a dangerous thing, not so much because you may make mistakes about them, but because you may be revealing the truth about yourself.
JUDGE HAROLD MEDINA

Hesitancy in judgment is the only true mark of the thinker.
DAGOBERT D. RUNES

Hero Worship

Live a life filled with love, following the example of Christ. He loved us and offered himself as a sacrifice for us, a pleasing aroma to God.
EPHESIANS 5:2

LAUREN NOTICED ABSOLUTELY everything Savannah did. She watched to see how Savannah moved her hands when she was talking. She listened to things Savannah said and added those phrases to her own conversations. She dressed like Savannah and wore her hair like Savannah. She did everything she could to be just like Savannah. Lauren noticed who Savannah talked to and who she ignored. When Savannah made fun of someone, Lauren did too. She liked the same activities, same music, same movies. She wanted to be exactly like Savannah. In fact, Lauren was a little clone of Savannah.

When Savannah was making good choices and being a kind person, Lauren was too. But when Savannah treated other people poorly or made unwise choices, Lauren's hero worship got her into trouble. Sometimes being just like Savannah was not a good thing.

While there is sometimes a temptation to model yourself after someone you admire, that should never be taken to an extreme. God makes each person unique; he doesn't need two copies of the same person. God made you to be just the way he wants you to be. And the reality is that no person can live up to being someone's hero, because no one is perfect. All people occasionally make bad choices or lose their tempers or say things they later regret.

There is only one person who is worthy of becoming your hero. That person is Jesus, of course. The Bible records stories of how Jesus treated people and how he acted and reacted to situations while he was here on earth. In the Bible you will find everything you need to know about how to model your life after his. You may have to think a little to figure out how Jesus would act in the typical situations you face. But there is enough information about him to know how he would handle just about everything you have to deal with. Jesus loved people unconditionally. He was kind and helpful. He was honest and always true to his character. Jesus loved God first, and he loved other people next.

Hero worship isn't such a bad idea . . . if you make Jesus your hero. The more you model your life after his, the more you will please and obey God, and the more your relationships with others will be filled with love.

CHECKUP TIME

On a scale of 1 to 5, how are you dealing with hero worship?

1 = never
2 = not very often
3 = sometimes
4 = most of the time
5 = always

I have high standards when choosing people I admire.

1   2   3   4   5

I copy my life after Jesus.

1   2   3   4   5

I know younger girls may be watching me, so I'm careful to be a good role model.

1   2   3   4   5

I read the Bible to find out more about how Jesus lived.

1   2   3   4   5

It's important to me to show God's love to others.

1   2   3   4   5

KEY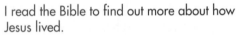

MOSTLY 1s Your hero worship is out of control. Choose one area from the statements above to work on.

MOSTLY 2s You may be choosing poor role models. Think about how you can change that.

MOSTLY 3s Come on, you can do better.

MOSTLY 4s You know who your only hero should be, but you can still work harder at living like him.

MOSTLY 5s Wonderful! You are modeling Jesus to the world around you!

THINGS TO DO

☐ Make a list of people you look up to and the qualities about them you admire. Are there things you shouldn't worry so much about imitating? Are there things you should be imitating but aren't?

☐ Keep track for one week of how much time you spend reading your Bible. Is there some way you can make your time with God more consistent?

☐ Ask God how you can show someone his love this week.

☐ Think about the young girls in your life who may be copying you. Is there something about your behavior that needs to change with this in mind?

THINGS TO REMEMBER

I am the light of the world. If you follow me, you won't have to walk in darkness, because you will have the light that leads to life. **JOHN 8:12**

Don't copy the behavior and customs of this world, but let God transform you into a new person by changing the way you think. Then you will learn to know God's will for you, which is good and pleasing and perfect. **ROMANS 12:2**

May you always be filled with the fruit of your salvation—the righteous character produced in your life by Jesus Christ—for this will bring much glory and praise to God. **PHILIPPIANS 1:11**

Dear friend, don't let this bad example influence you. Follow only what is good. Remember that those who do good prove that they are God's children, and those who do evil prove that they do not know God. **3 JOHN 1:11**

Just as you accepted Christ Jesus as your Lord, you must continue to follow him. **COLOSSIANS 2:6**

Whatever your heart clings to and confides in, that is really your God.
MARTIN LUTHER

You become like those who you idealize, admire, and follow.
UNKNOWN

Jesus Christ is the center of everything, and the object of everything, and he that does not know Him knows nothing of the order of nature and nothing of himself.
BLAISE PASCAL

Out of Patience

A hot-tempered person starts fights; a cool-tempered person stops them.
PROVERBS 15:18

"ARE WE GOING to sit here all day? Can't we go?" Mia whined. She really didn't like it when the family sat around the table at the restaurant and chatted. Her mom reminded her that it was a good chance for family members to connect, and she encouraged Mia to join in the conversation. But the only thing Mia would say is, "Can we go now?" She made everyone so uncomfortable that finally everyone got up and went home.

And that's not the only time Mia got impatient. She couldn't stand it when a friend wanted to tell her something but took forever to get the information out. "Just spit it out!" she shouted. She just didn't have time for all the extra details that go into telling a story.

Mia has a real problem with patience . . . she doesn't have much. It makes people (even her friends) nervous to be around her because something they say or do often sets her off and she starts yelling at them. It's hard to spend much time with someone like that.

What's the deal with impatience? Why are some people so consumed by it? Actually, impatience is an expression of self-centeredness. An impatient person is convinced that everyone needs to play by her rules and agree with her about what's important. She doesn't care about other people's feelings or what's going on in their lives. She's only concerned about herself and wants everyone else to do what she wants.

An impatient person is disobeying one very important command God gave: to love others as you love yourself. When you love others, you care about what's going on in their lives and what's important to them. It's certainly the way Jesus lived. He put others' needs ahead of his own, no matter how tired or busy he was. And he was patient and caring with everyone who came to him. Jesus' patience is a good model of how we can connect with other people and show them love.

CHECKUP TIME

On a scale of 1 to 5, how's your patience level?

1 = never
2 = not very often
3 = sometimes
4 = most of the time
5 = always

I listen to other people's opinions and ideas.
1   2   3   4   5

I submit to others instead of insisting on having my own way.
1   2   3   4   5

I value other people and their needs.
1   2   3   4   5

Jesus is my model for relationships.
1   2   3   4   5

I show God's love to others in the way I treat them.
1   2   3   4   5

KEY

MOSTLY 1s Patience is not your strong point. Choose one thing from the quiz to start working on.

MOSTLY 2s You can definitely do better than this.

MOSTLY 3s Middle of the road—there's room to grow.

MOSTLY 4s You're pretty patient, but there's room for improvement.

MOSTLY 5s Good job. You are modeling Jesus' patience to the world around you!

THINGS TO DO

- ☐ Ask a friend to tell you honestly how you're doing in the patience department. Are there certain areas she sees room where you can improve?

- ☐ Think of three ways you can show kindness and patience to others this week.

- ☐ Think about the times you've been impatient recently. What do you think caused your short temper? Confess your impatience to God, and apologize to people who you may have hurt.

- ☐ Ask God to help you be more patient and value others more in the future.

THINGS TO REMEMBER

Better to be patient than powerful; better to have self-control than to conquer a city.
PROVERBS 16:32

May God, who gives this patience and encouragement, help you live in complete harmony with each other, as is fitting for followers of Christ Jesus. **ROMANS 15:5**

Always be humble and gentle. Be patient with each other, making allowance for each other's faults because of your love. **EPHESIANS 4:2**

Be patient with everyone. **1 THESSALONIANS 5:14**

You, too, must be patient. Take courage, for the coming of the Lord is near. **JAMES 5:8**

One moment of patience may ward off great disaster. One moment of impatience may ruin a whole life.
CHINESE PROVERB

Patience and time do more than strength or passion.
JEAN DE LA FONTAINE

Adopt the pace of nature: her secret is patience.
RALPH WALDO EMERSON

Not My Kind

Don't forget to show hospitality to strangers, for some who have done this have entertained angels without realizing it!
HEBREWS 13:2

"I SIT?" MARIA motioned with her lunch tray to the chair beside Aidyn. Without even giving it a second thought, Aidyn shook her head and put her books on the seat. Then she looked around, hoping her friends would rescue her. Maria looked embarrassed and walked away. *Whew,* Aidyn thought. *I dodged that one—why would she even want to sit beside me? She barely speaks English. Even if she did, what would we have to talk about? We're waaay different from each other!*

What Aidyn doesn't know is that Maria's family had to leave behind everything familiar when they came to the United States hoping for a better life. Aidyn hasn't taken the time to learn Maria's story—why her family came, what their homeland is like, or how they are adjusting to life in a completely new culture and a different language.

Aidyn is prejudiced. There are many different kinds of prejudice, and it can come out in different ways—everything from making rude comments and jokes about another race to judging someone based on her culture or background. Whatever form it comes in, prejudice is the opinion that a group of people is less important or less valuable than your group. Not very biblical. You won't find any verse that says, "God loves people from North America best" or "God loves only people who have nice homes and go to church." Nope, the Bible says, "God loved the world." That means people of all nationalities and backgrounds.

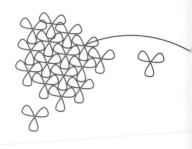

The Bible tells us that the world will know you are different from those who don't know Christ because of the love you show to those around you. Christ's love is not limited to people who seem to have it all together—in fact, he often sought out the poor and those who didn't seem to fit in well with society. Prejudice and love can't live in the same place. If your heart is consumed with prejudice against any group of people, you are not showing Christ's love to the world. If God loves the world—and all kinds of people—so much, surely he wants us to do the same.

CHECKUP TIME

On a scale of 1 to 5, what's your prejudice rate?

1 = never
2 = not very often
3 = sometimes
4 = most of the time
5 = always

I am friendly to people at school and in my neighborhood, no matter where they're from.
1   2   3   4   5

I like to meet people from other countries.
1   2   3   4   5

It's interesting to me to learn new things about other cultures.
1   2   3   4   5

I am sympathetic to people who had to leave their countries.
1   2   3   4   5

I believe God made everyone equally valuable and special.
1   2   3   4   5

KEY

MOSTLY 1s You'd better get to work on your attitude of prejudice. Choose one thing from the list above to tackle this week.

MOSTLY 2s Not so good. You have some work to do.

MOSTLY 3s Average, but there's room to grow.

MOSTLY 4s You're pretty compassionate and kind, but there's room for improvement.

MOSTLY 5s Good job. You are showing Christ's love to all.

THINGS TO DO

☐ Get to know someone from your school, church, or neighborhood who is from another country.

☐ Read up on the country that person is from.

☐ Learn a few words of her language.

☐ Encourage your friends to be kinder to those who are different.

THINGS TO REMEMBER

You must not mistreat or oppress foreigners in any way. **EXODUS 22:21**

I was hungry, and you fed me. I was thirsty, and you gave me a drink. I was a stranger, and you invited me into your home. **MATTHEW 25:35**

True justice must be given to foreigners living among you. **DEUTERONOMY 24:17**

The LORD protects the foreigners among us. **PSALM 146:9**

I saw a vast crowd, too great to count, from every nation and tribe and people and language, standing in front of the throne and before the Lamb. **REVELATION 7:9**

Let us all hope that the dark clouds of racial prejudice will soon pass away . . . and in some not too distant tomorrow the radiant stars of love and brotherhood will shine over our great nation.
MARTIN LUTHER KING JR.

If there is anything better than to be loved it is loving.
ANONYMOUS

I have found the paradox that if I love until it hurts, then there is no hurt but only more love.
MOTHER TERESA

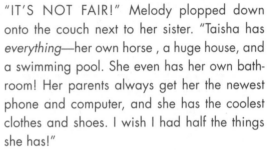

Green with Envy

Love is not jealous.
1 CORINTHIANS 13:4

"IT'S NOT FAIR!" Melody plopped down onto the couch next to her sister. "Taisha has *everything*—her own horse , a huge house, and a swimming pool. She even has her own bathroom! Her parents always get her the newest phone and computer, and she has the coolest clothes and shoes. I wish I had half the things she has!"

Whoa! Melody is green with envy. That's kind of a strange expression, but it just means that Melody is totally jealous of Taisha's stuff. Jealousy starts as a little itch in your heart—like when you notice a friend's cool phone or awesome boots. But it's the kind of heart disease that grows and grows. If you don't do something to keep it in check, it gets completely out of control. When that happens, friendships can be wrecked and people's testimonies of living for God can be damaged. No good can come of that.

Jealousy, like most other sins, comes right back to the problem of selfishness and self-centeredness. Being jealous of someone's stuff or success shows that you're thinking mostly about yourself and what you have or how others view you. You are driven by the need to be more successful and more important than anyone else. When this desire gets out of control, it leads you to do ugly things, like spread rumors about the person you're jealous of or try to get her other friends to drop her. Not a pretty scene.

A person who conquers her jealousy is able to celebrate with her friends when they get new stuff or when they have successes in their lives. Think about it—you like it when your friends celebrate with you, right? So it only makes sense that your friends would enjoy that too. God's desire is for you to love your friends with all your heart—there is no room for jealousy and love in the same heart. So ask God to set your heart free from the jealousy that's controlling it.

CHECKUP TIME

On a scale of 1 to 5, how's your jealousy quotient?

1 = never
2 = not very often
3 = sometimes
4 = most of the time
5 = always

I am thankful for what I've been given.

1   2   3   4   5

I sincerely celebrate my friends' successes with them.

1   2   3   4   5

I am happy for my friends when they get new things.

1   2   3   4   5

I am content with the opportunities and circumstances God has given me.

1   2   3   4   5

I confess my feelings of jealousy to God when I feel them creeping into my heart.

1   2   3   4   5

KEY

MOSTLY 1s Your skin is *green*. Start working on your jealousy issues.

MOSTLY 2s Yikes! You care more about yourself than others.

MOSTLY 3s So-so, but you can do better.

MOSTLY 4s You're doing pretty well, but there is room for improvement.

MOSTLY 5s Great! You're a selfless friend who celebrates with others.

THINGS TO DO

☐ Write down a list of things that make you jealous. Are your feelings of jealousy hurting any of your relationships?

☐ Make a list of things you have to be thankful for.

☐ Make it a point to congratulate someone on an accomplishment or success this week.

☐ Ask God to help you be more loving and less jealous.

THINGS TO REMEMBER

I observed that most people are motivated to success because they envy their neighbors. But this, too, is meaningless—like chasing the wind. **ECCLESIASTES 4:4**

You are still controlled by your sinful nature. You are jealous of one another and quarrel with each other. Doesn't that prove you are controlled by your sinful nature? Aren't you living like people of the world? **1 CORINTHIANS 3:3**

Since we are living by the Spirit, let us follow the Spirit's leading in every part of our lives. Let us not become conceited, or provoke one another, or be jealous of one another. **GALATIANS 5:25-26**

If you are bitterly jealous and there is selfish ambition in your heart, don't cover up the truth with boasting and lying. For jealousy and selfishness are not God's kind of wisdom. Such things are earthly, unspiritual, and demonic. **JAMES 3:14-15**

Envy is the art of counting the other fellow's blessings instead of your own.
HAROLD COFFIN

You can never get enough of what you don't need to make you happy.
ERIC HOFFER

Love is not about getting, but giving.
HENRY VAN DYKE

I Am the Greatest!

Pride ends in humiliation, while humility brings honor.
PROVERBS 29:23

HANNAH GRABBED a basketball and ran onto the court. She dribbled up and down the gym floor, making layups at each end. Other girls stood on the sidelines and watched her. Hannah seemed to glide through the air. She flew high and effortlessly as she tossed the ball into the hoop. Nothing but net. There was no doubt Hannah was the best basketball player on the girls' team—maybe even better than most of the guys, too.

Hannah liked the attention. She knew she was a good athlete, and it made her feel good to hear other people acknowledge her skills. In fact, one of her favorite things to do besides play basketball was to talk about it—her best games and the awesome shots she'd made. She loved it when other people joined in the conversation and praised her skills. She was plenty proud of the star power her basketball abilities gave her.

As you might have guessed, humility is not Hannah's strongest quality. Someone who likes to talk about herself and how good she is at something is filled with pride, not humility. And Hannah's desire to hear other people sing her praises shows that she has a problem with thinking too highly of herself.

Now, it's okay to acknowledge that God has given you a talent in something and even to work hard to improve your skills. But talking about how good you are or feeling that others could not possibly be as good as you are crosses the line into pride. There is a fine line separating an awareness of the abilities God gave you and taking credit for them yourself.

Think about Jesus for a minute. He was God—actual God. If that's not something to be proud of, then what would be? But Jesus wasn't filled with pride. In fact, he came to earth and lived the humble life of a simple teacher. He served people and helped them instead of expecting others to serve him. He didn't brag about being God or how much power he had. He served others in love. Jesus is the perfect model of humility.

CHECKUP TIME

On a scale of 1 to 5, how's your humility?

1 = never
2 = not very often
3 = sometimes
4 = most of the time
5 = always

I compliment my friends on their abilities.
1   2   3   4   5

I listen to other people instead of just talking about myself.
1   2   3   4   5

I give God the credit for my abilities.
1   2   3   4   5

I recognize that God has given each person gifts and talents.
1   2   3   4   5

I work hard to improve my skills.
1   2   3   4   5

KEY

MOSTLY 1s Humility isn't your strong point. Choose one area to work on from the quiz above.

MOSTLY 2s Come on, you can do better than this.

MOSTLY 3s Middle of the road—sometimes humble, sometimes proud.

MOSTLY 4s Okay, but there is room for improvement.

MOSTLY 5s Good job giving God the credit.

THINGS TO DO

☐ Pay attention to all your conversations for one entire day. Do you talk about yourself a lot?

☐ Compliment one person each day on his or her abilities.

☐ Think about the areas where you are most talented. Then thank God for giving you those abilities.

☐ Ask God to help you be more humble, modeling Jesus to others.

THINGS TO REMEMBER

Pride leads to disgrace, but with humility comes wisdom. **PROVERBS 11:2**

Though [Jesus] was God, he did not think of equality with God as something to cling to. Instead, he gave up his divine privileges; he took the humble position of a slave and was born as a human being. **PHILIPPIANS 2:6-7**

All of you, serve each other in humility, for "God opposes the proud but favors the humble."
1 PETER 5:5

I, the LORD, will punish the world for its evil and the wicked for their sin. I will crush the arrogance of the proud and humble the pride of the mighty.
ISAIAH 13:11

There are different kinds of spiritual gifts, but the same Spirit is the source of them all.
1 CORINTHIANS 12:4

Some people are born on third base and go through life thinking they hit a triple.
BARRY SWITZER

None are so empty as those who are full of themselves.
BENJAMIN WHICHCOTE

Pride makes us artificial, and humility makes us real.
THOMAS MERTON

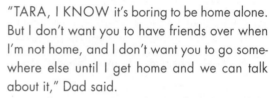

As Long as I Don't Get Caught

Those who obey God's word truly show how completely they love him. That is how we know we are living in him.
1 JOHN 2:5

"TARA, I KNOW it's boring to be home alone. But I don't want you to have friends over when I'm not home, and I don't want you to go somewhere else until I get home and we can talk about it," Dad said.

"Dad, come on," Tara begged. "I just want to go to Stefanie's house. No big deal. I don't want to wait until you get home from work."

"No. I don't know Stefanie or her family. I'm sorry I don't get home from work earlier— believe me, I wish I did. But that's the way it is. That's the rule at our house: stay home until I get there. End of discussion."

The next afternoon Tara didn't come home after school. She went to Stefanie's house instead. She deliberately disobeyed her dad. She thought she could get away with it by making sure she was back before her dad came home.

So does disobedience only count if you get caught? That would be nice, wouldn't it? But that's not the way it works. Tara had two strikes against her right away. One, she disobeyed her dad. He told her what the rule was, plain and simple, and she broke it. Second, she planned out her disobedience ahead of time. She purposely went against his expectations.

Whether or not Tara got caught was not really the issue. Disobedience is a flat-out sin, and even if her dad never found out about it, there is someone who already knew: God.

Yep, there are no secrets from him, and he is the one who said obedience is the only way. God makes it clear that it's important to obey not only him but also the people who are in authority over you. So you have to think about obeying parents, teachers, and coaches, not just God himself. Obedience to rules and laws and people in authority is what gives order to our world. If you have an attitude and a lifestyle of obedience, you won't have to worry about getting caught for anything.

CHECKUP TIME

On a scale of 1 to 5, how are you doing at obedience?

1 = never
2 = not very often
3 = sometimes
4 = most of the time
5 = always

I obey the rules set up by my parents and teachers.
1   2   3   4   5

If I do disobey, I own up to it instead of trying to hide it.
1   2   3   4   5

I accept the rules I've been given.
1   2   3   4   5

I choose friends who respect the rules.
1   2   3   4   5

I obey the rules God has set up in the Bible.
1   2   3   4   5

KEY

MOSTLY 1s Obedience is not your strong point. How can you begin working on this in your life?

MOSTLY 2s Well, you're not the most disobedient person ever, but you've got a long way to go.

MOSTLY 3s Middle of the road—which is not good enough. You can do better.

MOSTLY 4s You obey most of the time, but there is room for improvement.

MOSTLY 5s Good job choosing obedience.

THINGS TO DO

- ☐ Think about the areas where you have the most trouble obeying. Ask God for his help in becoming more obedient in these areas.

- ☐ Memorize a verse about being obedient, such as Ephesians 6:1 or Hebrews 13:17.

- ☐ Encourage your friends to be obedient and honoring to their parents and other authority figures in their lives.

- ☐ Think about someone you have disobeyed recently and apologize to that person.

THINGS TO REMEMBER

Anyone who hears my teaching and doesn't obey it is foolish, like a person who builds a house on sand.
MATTHEW 7:26

Children, always obey your parents, for this pleases the Lord. **COLOSSIANS 3:20**

My son, obey your father's commands, and don't neglect your mother's instruction. **PROVERBS 6:20**

Obey your spiritual leaders, and do what they say. Their work is to watch over your souls, and they are accountable to God. Give them reason to do this with joy and not with sorrow. That would certainly not be for your benefit. **HEBREWS 13:17**

Those who accept my commandments and obey them are the ones who love me. And because they love me, my Father will love them. And I will love them and reveal myself to each of them.
JOHN 14:21

Wicked men obey from fear; good men, from love.
ARISTOTLE

True obedience is true freedom.
HENRY WARD BEECHER

A child who is allowed to be disrespectful to his parents will not have true respect for anyone.
BILLY GRAHAM

Keep On Keeping On

EVERY DAY OF the week Mallory went straight from school to her gymnastics club, where she worked out for several hours. Some days she worked on her uneven bar routine until her hands were bleeding. But she just wrapped them and kept on working. Bruises, pulled muscles, shin splints . . . these things might have slowed her down, but they didn't stop her. She knew that constant practice was the only way to get better. And she did get better, improving her skills and winning awards. She persevered through extreme physical training so she could be a better athlete.

Perseverance is the decision to keep on keeping on. It's a choice to keep working and trying, no matter how difficult things get. The best athletes are experts at perseverance because, like Mallory, they work their muscles to learn new skills, and they push through pain and injury to get better.

There is another area where perseverance is important, whether you're an athlete or not. Perseverance is necessary in the Christian life too—in living a life of faith that honors and obeys God. It may seem like the Christian life is a piece of cake. You go to church and youth group, read your Bible once in a while, and pray when you think of it. No big deal, right?

Wrong. You should know that once you begin trying to live for God, Satan is going to throw every roadblock he can think of in your way. The first steps of living for God are baby steps. But as you continue to learn and grow in your faith, the next steps can get harder because they are a bit more involved. As you go deeper in your faith, it takes perseverance to keep on going when things get harder. And just as an athlete gets better results from her body as she keeps working out, God wants you to commit to becoming more and more like Christ. He will help you as you keep working through the hard times and trusting him more.

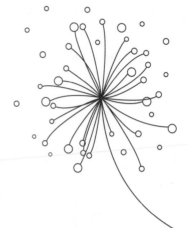

CHECKUP TIME

On a scale of 1 to 5, how's your perseverance?

1 = never
2 = not very often
3 = sometimes
4 = most of the time
5 = always

I keep working, no matter how hard things get.

1   2   3   4   5

I set goals for myself and then do what it takes to accomplish them.

1   2   3   4   5

I encourage my friends to keep on keeping on.

1   2   3   4   5

I am committed to becoming more and more like Christ.

1   2   3   4   5

I believe good results are worth the pain and effort.

1   2   3   4   5

KEY

MOSTLY 1s You need to commit to working harder. Choose one area you can focus on.

MOSTLY 2s You're taking the easy way out. Come on, you can do it!

MOSTLY 3s So-so. See if you can try harder.

MOSTLY 4s Not bad, but there is room for improvement.

MOSTLY 5s Congratulations! You are a hard worker.

THINGS TO DO

- ☐ Make a list of some of the hard things about living for God. Then ask God to give you perseverance as you face those challenges.

- ☐ Write down three goals you want to accomplish, and start working toward at least one of them today.

- ☐ Read your Bible and pray every day. God gives us encouragement and strength through his Word.

- ☐ Ask a friend or a mentor to pray that you'll keep on keeping on in a certain area of your life.

THINGS TO REMEMBER

I don't mean to say that I have already achieved these things or that I have already reached perfection. But I press on to possess that perfection for which Christ Jesus first possessed me.
PHILIPPIANS 3:12

I press on to reach the end of the race and receive the heavenly prize for which God, through Christ Jesus, is calling us. **PHILIPPIANS 3:14**

The LORD will work out his plans for my life— for your faithful love, O LORD, endures forever.
PSALM 138:8

This will continue until we all come to such unity in our faith and knowledge of God's Son that we will be mature in the Lord, measuring up to the full and complete standard of Christ. **EPHESIANS 4:13**

Oh, that we might know the LORD! Let us press on to know him. **HOSEA 6:3**

Many of the great achievements of the world were accomplished by tired and discouraged men who kept on working.
UNKNOWN

Edison failed 10,000 times before he made the electric light. Do not be discouraged if you fail a few times.
NAPOLEON HILL

By perseverance the snail reached the ark.
CHARLES H. SPURGEON

Why Not?

*Temptation comes
from our own desires,
which entice us and
drag us away.*
JAMES 1:14

"IT'S SIMPLE," Mary said. "You sneak into your mom's purse and find her credit card. Then you go online, set up an account, and buy anything you want." She spread out the stack of movies that had just arrived in the mail. "Have them delivered to my address, then I'll just tell my mom that a friend bought them as a surprise for someone and that's why they come here. No big deal." Taylor had to admit that it did sound simple.

"But what happens when the charge shows up on my mom's credit card bill?" Taylor asked.

"Just keep quiet. She'll figure the credit card company made a mistake and then complain to them. They'll take the charge off—and you get the movies for free. No one gets hurt," Mary said. "Try it. You can get all kinds of stuff. Do you know where your mom's credit card is?" Taylor was tempted. It sounded so easy, and if no one got hurt, well, why not?

Temptation always makes things look easy and attractive. If it didn't, you wouldn't be tempted, right? It can take a lot of strength to resist temptation sometimes. You might wonder, *If no one would ever find out that I gave in to temptation and did something wrong, what's the big deal?*

Here's the big deal: Even if no one else knows what you've done, even if your action is never discovered, even if you can lie your way out of trouble . . . God knows what you've done. There are no secrets from him. And there is also no temptation you have to fight that he doesn't understand. That's the cool thing about Jesus coming to earth as a human. He faced temptation, and he fought it off. Satan tempted Jesus for forty days straight, offering power, success, and physical satisfaction, but Jesus did not give in at all. He knows what you're going through, and he'll help you face it.

CHECKUP TIME

On a scale of 1 to 5, how are you handling temptation?

1 = never
2 = not very often
3 = sometimes
4 = most of the time
5 = always

I resist temptation, even when it's difficult.
1   2   3   4   5

When I'm really tempted, I get help.
1   2   3   4   5

I believe that wrong is wrong, even if no one knows about it.
1   2   3   4   5

I ask God to help me fight temptation.
1   2   3   4   5

When I do give in to temptation, I confess what I've done instead of lying about it.
1   2   3   4   5

KEY

MOSTLY 1s Whoa, you may be strong, but not when it comes to fighting temptation.

MOSTLY 2s You have a little start, but it's time to learn more about how to fight temptation.

MOSTLY 3s Uhh, you're not going to win any awards. You can do better.

MOSTLY 4s Not bad, but you could put up a stronger fight against temptation.

MOSTLY 5s Good job. You are a temptation resister!

THINGS TO DO

- ☐ Make a list of the areas where you're often tempted to sin.

- ☐ Make a list of ways to fight each kind of temptation you face.

- ☐ Think about whether any of the people you hang out with encourage you to give in to temptation. If so, it may be time to choose some new friends.

- ☐ Memorize a verse that you can say when you are facing temptation, such as 1 Corinthians 10:13 or Hebrews 4:15.

THINGS TO REMEMBER

The Spirit then compelled Jesus to go into the wilderness, where he was tempted by Satan for forty days. **MARK 1:12-13**

Keep watch and pray, so that you will not give in to temptation. For the spirit is willing, but the body is weak! **MATTHEW 26:41**

The temptations in your life are no different from what others experience. And God is faithful. He will not allow the temptation to be more than you can stand. When you are tempted, he will show you a way out so that you can endure.
1 CORINTHIANS 10:13

God blesses those who patiently endure testing and temptation. Afterward they will receive the crown of life that God has promised to those who love him. **JAMES 1:12**

This High Priest of ours understands our weaknesses, for he faced all of the same testings we do, yet he did not sin. **HEBREWS 4:15**

'Tis one thing to be tempted. . . . Another thing to fall.
WILLIAM SHAKESPEARE, FROM *MEASURE FOR MEASURE*

Temptation is not sin, but playing with temptation invites sin.
UNKNOWN

Stand with anybody that stands right, stand with him while he is right and part with him when he goes wrong.
ABRAHAM LINCOLN

Stressed Out!

The LORD gives his people strength. The LORD blesses them with peace.
PSALM 29:11

ALEXA'S HEART WAS racing. Her breath came in short, shallow gasps. Her hands were sweaty and cold. Why? The piano. Yep, Alexa had been asked to play the piano for the Christmas Eve service at church. She'd said yes (mostly because her mom had encouraged her to), but now she was so stressed about it that she was nearly sick. *It's not going to be cool if I sit down at the piano and pass out or throw up in front of the whole church,* she kept telling herself. But she didn't know what to do. She was scared to play and scared not to play. Well, that didn't make any sense. Maybe it was more like this: she wanted to play, but she would give anything in the world to not have to play. Sigh. There was no doubt about it—she was just stressed about the whole thing.

Stress is a real response to difficult situations, and it can really mess things up. When you're stressed, your mind can't seem to concentrate on anything except what you're stressed about and the what-ifs that go with it. *What if I mess up? What if people don't like it? What if someone makes fun of me?* Stress makes you unable to think about things from another person's perspective. Stress makes you "you-focused."

So how do you deal with stress? There's a double answer to that. First, you need to ask God to help you. And yes, he will help you. But you have some responsibility too. You need to slow down and make space for God to give you strength and courage. That means your job is to stop panicking, take a few deep breaths, and concentrate on God's presence in your life right now. Spend time reading his Word and praying so you can connect with him and find his peace and rest. God will work in your heart, but you have to be tuned in to him so you can benefit from his presence in your life.

CHECKUP TIME

On a scale of 1 to 5, how do you handle stress?

I know how to deal with stress so it doesn't take over my life.
1   2   3   4   5

1 = never
2 = not very often
3 = sometimes
4 = most of the time
5 = always

I can quiet the swirling inside and listen for God's voice.
1   2   3   4   5

When I'm stressing, I talk to God.
1   2   3   4   5

I believe that God is present in my life.
1   2   3   4   5

When I'm stressed, I try to think about others and what they're going through.
1   2   3   4   5

KEY

MOSTLY 1s Stress seems to have control of you.

MOSTLY 2s Stress is tiring—choose one area to work on to lessen its control over you.

MOSTLY 3s Come on, you can do better.

MOSTLY 4s Not bad, but you could be more calm.

MOSTLY 5s Great—stress is under control in your life.

THINGS TO DO

☐ Make a list of the things that cause you stress. Think about why they stress you out.

☐ Make a list of things you can do that help you handle stress, such as exercise, prayer, and planning ahead.

☐ Think about how you treat others when you're stressed. Apologize to anyone you might have been impatient with recently as a result of stress.

☐ Ask God to help you overcome the stress in your life.

THINGS TO REMEMBER

Those who love your instructions have great peace and do not stumble. **PSALM 119:165**

All who listen to me will live in peace, untroubled by fear of harm. **PROVERBS 1:33**

You will keep in perfect peace all who trust in you, all whose thoughts are fixed on you! **ISAIAH 26:3**

Those who live in the shelter of the Most High will find rest in the shadow of the Almighty. **PSALM 91:1**

Take my yoke upon you. Let me teach you, because I am humble and gentle at heart, and you will find rest for your souls. **MATTHEW 11:29**

Peace is not the absence of conflict, but the ability to cope with it.
UNKNOWN

In times of stress, be bold and valiant.
HORACE

Be not afraid of life. Believe that life is worth living, and your belief will help create the fact.
WILLIAM JAMES

Getting Even

CARISSA SAT AT her desk with a notebook in front of her. She tapped her pencil on her desk as she thought. Finally, she furiously began to scribble a list onto the page. Once in a while a wicked smile crossed her face. *I will make Brianna sorry for this!* Carissa thought. She was making a list of ways she could get even with her friend (well, former friend) Brianna.

Carissa had told Brianna who she liked. She really didn't want the whole world to know about it, but Brianna had gone and blabbed it to everyone she met. Other people at school were coming up to Carissa and teasing her about it or laughing at her behind her back. Carissa went straight to Brianna and asked if she had told her secret. Brianna didn't even try to hide it. She just said, "Chill. It's no big deal." Well, it was a big deal to Carissa, and she was determined to make Brianna pay!

It's understandable that Carissa was angry and hurt that Brianna spilled her secret. It hurts when someone you trusted lets you down. She did the right thing by talking to Brianna about it, but it must have hurt even more when Brianna didn't take the problem seriously. There's a better solution than getting even. The desire to get revenge can quickly take over your life, and it really has no good results—for the other person or for you.

Carissa can hurt Brianna, but all that does

is absolutely ensure that their friendship is wrecked for good. It also makes Carissa look bad to other people. They will see that she is angry and vengeful inside. And even though Carissa thinks getting even will make her feel better, it will actually end up making her miserable. But the biggest reason not to seek revenge is because God says it's wrong to deliberately hurt or embarrass someone else. Even though Brianna hurt her, Carissa needs to remember that two wrongs don't make a right. She doesn't have to tell Brianna any more secrets, but she doesn't need to get even with her either. Forgiveness is the best answer to what Brianna did. That will show the love that God instructed his children to have for one another.

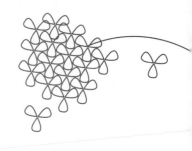

CHECKUP TIME

On a scale of 1 to 5, how do you approach revenge?

1 = never
2 = not very often
3 = sometimes
4 = most of the time
5 = always

When someone hurts me, I forgive that person, with no plans for getting even.
1   2   3   4   5

I can move on after someone has hurt me, without holding a grudge.
1   2   3   4   5

My friends see me as kind and forgiving.
1   2   3   4   5

I believe it is important to show God's love to others.
1   2   3   4   5

I am considerate toward others, being careful not to hurt or embarrass them.
1   2   3   4   5

KEY

MOSTLY 1s Whoa, is *revenge* your middle name? Choose an area to work on to start becoming a more forgiving person.

MOSTLY 2s Getting even takes a lot of energy—can't you put your energy somewhere else?

MOSTLY 3s So-so. You can do better.

MOSTLY 4s Not bad, but keep working on letting go of your anger.

MOSTLY 5s Love, not revenge, is your focus. Keep it up!

THINGS TO DO

☐ Think about the last time you were hurt by someone. How did you respond? What will you do differently if you face a situation like that again?

☐ Apologize to someone you have deliberately hurt or ignored.

☐ Ask God to fill your heart with love for those around you.

☐ Think about a person you're holding a grudge against or someone you're tempted to get even with. Make a decision to forgive that person with God's help.

THINGS TO REMEMBER

Dear friends, never take revenge. Leave that to the righteous anger of God. For the Scriptures say, "I will take revenge; I will pay them back," says the LORD. **ROMANS 12:19**

Forgive us our sins, as we forgive those who sin against us. **LUKE 11:4**

[Jesus] did not retaliate when he was insulted, nor threaten revenge when he suffered. He left his case in the hands of God, who always judges fairly. **1 PETER 2:23**

Do not seek revenge or bear a grudge . . . but love your neighbor as yourself. **LEVITICUS 19:18**

Jesus said, "Father, forgive them, for they don't know what they are doing." **LUKE 23:34**

Revenge is often like biting a dog because the dog bit you.
AUSTIN O'MALLEY

There is no revenge so complete as forgiveness.
JOSH BILLINGS

Revenge has no more quenching effect on emotions than salt water has on thirst.
WALTER WECKLER

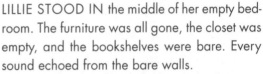

Saying Good-Bye

May the LORD keep watch between you and me when we are away from each other.
GENESIS 31:49 (NIV)

LILLIE STOOD IN the middle of her empty bedroom. The furniture was all gone, the closet was empty, and the bookshelves were bare. Every sound echoed from the bare walls.

"Let's go, Lil," Mom called up the stairs.

But Lillie didn't move. As she looked around the room, memories of times with friends flooded her mind: Late-night talks with her best friend, Suzie. Laughter, secrets, tears. Painting their nails, trying new hairstyles, doing all the things that bond friends together and make life special. Lillie remembered the pictures that used to be pinned on her wall and the awards and notes from school and youth group activities. There was a knot in Lillie's stomach. She was going to miss her friends. Even if she made new friends in their new town, no one would ever replace Suzie. They had been best friends for five years, and they shared so many memories.

"Lil, come on. Everyone else is in the car," Mom called again.

Lillie took one last look around the room before slowly walking out and pulling the door closed behind her. She started down the stairs, and when she reached the bottom . . . there was Suzie! They locked into the biggest hug ever.

"I promise we'll still talk every day," Suzie said. "My mom says I can come visit you, and you'll come back here too. We'll have so much to talk about!"

Tears ran down Lillie's cheeks as she told her friend good-bye and got in the car. As they drove away, she could see Suzie standing at the edge of the driveway, waving. "Friends forever!" Lillie yelled out the window.

Moving away from everything familiar is so hard. But there's comfort in the knowledge that old friends stick around and new friends are eventually added in. And thanks to technology, it's much easier to stay in touch with people who are far away. Plus, no matter where you move to, you'll never be alone, because God is always with you. And the connection you have with other Christians means you have a family that is worldwide!

CHECKUP TIME

On a scale of 1 to 5, how do you handle saying good-bye?

1 = never
2 = not very often
3 = sometimes
4 = most of the time
5 = always

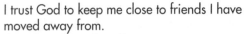

I look for the adventure when there are changes in my life.
1   2   3   4   5

I thank God for my friends—the ones who live near me and the ones who are far away.
1   2   3   4   5

I believe God is always with me.
1   2   3   4   5

I trust God to keep me close to friends I have moved away from.
1   2   3   4   5

I am open to making new friends.
1   2   3   4   5

KEY

MOSTLY 1s Saying good-bye is hard, but you need some work on your attitude.

MOSTLY 2s Choose one area from the quiz above to work on so you can be more open to change.

MOSTLY 3s Well, not bad, but you can do better.

MOSTLY 4s Okay, but you can still work on dealing with new situations.

MOSTLY 5s Good job—adventure and trust define your life.

FOR GIRLS ONLY
196

THINGS TO DO

☐ Think about good-byes you have had to say either because you moved or because a friend did. How did you handle them? Looking back, is there anything you would do differently next time?

☐ Think of a friend you've lost touch with. Write a note or an e-mail or give her a call to connect again.

☐ Make a list of good things that can come from changes in your life. How can you approach new circumstances as an adventure rather than a problem?

☐ Ask God to help you trust him for a good attitude toward change and for the persistence to stay in touch with friends.

THINGS TO REMEMBER

Go in peace, for we have sworn loyalty to each other in the LORD's name. The LORD is the witness of a bond between us. **1 SAMUEL 20:42**

When I am afraid, I will put my trust in you. **PSALM 56:3**

This world is not our permanent home; we are looking forward to a home yet to come. **HEBREWS 13:14**

So now you . . . are no longer strangers and foreigners. You are citizens along with all of God's holy people. You are members of God's family. **EPHESIANS 2:19**

Lord, through all the generations you have been our home! **PSALM 90:1**

Truly great friends are hard to find, difficult to leave, and impossible to forget.
UNKNOWN

If there ever comes a day when we can't be together, keep me in your heart. . . . I'll stay there forever.
WINNIE THE POOH

How lucky I am to have something that makes saying good-bye so hard.
ANNIE

Make It Stop!

Have compassion on me, LORD, for I am weak. Heal me, LORD, for my bones are in agony.
PSALM 6:2

"MY WHOLE LEG is throbbing," Nadia moaned. "It hurts so bad. Can't anyone make it stop? Please make it stop!"

Mom gave Nadia a sympathetic smile. "If I could make it stop, I would," she said. "I'm so sorry you have to go through this. The pain medication will help soon. In the meantime, let's see if we can think about some things that will make you feel better, okay?" Nadia didn't really want to, but she was willing to try anything to make the pain go away.

Mom sat down beside the bed and started recounting some of Nadia's biggest successes as a figure skater—competitions she had won and skills she had mastered. Mom even made Nadia smile once or twice as she recalled some of the fun times they had shared as they drove to practices and competitions around the area. Eventually Nadia started sharing some of her own favorite memories.

Pretty soon the pain wasn't so bad, and today's fall on the ice didn't seem so terrible. After all, the doctor had said her leg would heal and she would be able to continue the skating she loved so much.

Physical pain can be so consuming that it's hard to think about anything else. It's also hard to see past the pain to a time when life will continue in a normal way. So what do you do when you're in pain? You can curl up in a ball and just feel bad for yourself, or you can try to work through it and not focus on the pain.

It really helps to have someone to talk with to get your mind on other things when you're hurting. That's the joy of family and friends who care about you and encourage you. But remember that when you're in pain, it's okay to say so. It's okay to cry. And remember that you won't always feel like this. Try to occupy your mind with other things and thank God for the blessing of doctors and medicines that can help you through painful times. And thank him that someday, in heaven, there will be no more pain ever again.

CHECKUP TIME

On a scale of 1 to 5, how do you handle pain?

1 = never
2 = not very often
3 = sometimes
4 = most of the time
5 = always

When I am in pain, I try to be strong and work through it.
1   2   3   4   5

I let my friends and family encourage me when I'm hurt.
1   2   3   4   5

I thank God for doctors and medicine.
1   2   3   4   5

After I've recovered from pain or injury, I keep going and refuse to let it discourage me.
1   2   3   4   5

I believe that God promises us eternal healing in heaven someday.
1   2   3   4   5

KEY

MOSTLY 1s You don't handle pain well. You need to work on being stronger and letting God and others help you.

MOSTLY 2s Maybe you focus on pain too much. Try to think of encouraging things instead.

MOSTLY 3s Average. Try to improve your attitude.

MOSTLY 4s Okay, but there is room for improvement.

MOSTLY 5s Good job—pain doesn't get you down.

THINGS TO DO

- [ ] Think about the last time you were in pain. How did you handle it? What could you have done differently?
- [ ] Make a list of positive, encouraging things you can focus on the next time you're hurting.
- [ ] Visit someone at a hospital or in a nursing home who is experiencing pain. Think of a way you can encourage that person.
- [ ] Ask God for relief from pain, and thank him for his healing power.

THINGS TO REMEMBER

Are any of you sick? You should call for the elders of the church to come and pray over you, anointing you with oil in the name of the Lord. Such a prayer offered in faith will heal the sick, and the Lord will make you well. And if you have committed any sins, you will be forgiven.
JAMES 5:14-15

I am suffering and in pain. Rescue me, O God, by your saving power. **PSALM 69:29**

Because you are my helper, I sing for joy in the shadow of your wings. **PSALM 63:7**

We can say with confidence, "The LORD is my helper, so I will have no fear. What can mere people do to me?" **HEBREWS 13:6**

O LORD my God, I cried to you for help, and you restored my health. **PSALM 30:2**

The world is full of suffering; it is also full of overcoming it.
HELEN KELLER

The pain of the mind is worse than the pain of the body.
PUBLILIUS SYRUS

In time of sickness the soul collects itself anew.
LATIN PROVERB

Broken

The LORD is good,
a strong refuge when
trouble comes. He is
close to those who
trust in him.
NAHUM 1:7

CALLIE AND CHRIS huddled together in Callie's bedroom. Callie put her arm around her little brother's shoulders and held him close. They could hear their parents screaming at each other downstairs and the crashes of chairs and dishes being flung across the room. With each crash, Chris's little body shuddered. "It's okay. It's okay," Callie kept repeating. "It will be over in a minute."

But the fight lasted longer than usual. The two of them stayed quietly in Callie's room until they finally heard the front door slam and a car roar away. They waited a while, but no one came upstairs. Finally Callie said, "You stay here. I'll see what's going on."

"Don't go, Callie. Please don't go!" Chris begged.

"Shh. I'll be right back. I promise." Callie gave him a hug before she left.

She crept down the stairs. Broken chairs and dishes were scattered across the kitchen floor. Her mom was sitting at the table, sobbing. Callie would never let Chris know this, but she was scared.

The way God designed families is for parents to take care of their children and protect them from harm. But in some families, it doesn't happen like that. There's no doubt Callie and Chris wished that their mom and dad would get help and that there would be peace in their family. But that doesn't always happen either.

So what can Callie do? Number one, she can remember that God loves her and that he, too, is sad their family is broken and hurting. Next, she needs to understand that her parents' problems are not her fault. Callie's next step might be to find an adult who can help her and her brother by giving them a safe place to go or by encouraging their parents to go to counseling. God always provides someone to help, so Callie just needs to look around for that person and then trust God to help her. God cares for his children, and he will send someone to help you.

CHECKUP TIME

On a scale of 1 to 5, how do you handle family problems?

1 = never
2 = not very often
3 = sometimes
4 = most of the time
5 = always

I have people I can talk to when things are hard.
1   2   3   4   5

I believe God cares about what's happening in my family.
1   2   3   4   5

I go to someone for help when I need it.
1   2   3   4   5

I know I am loved.
1   2   3   4   5

I know my future is in God's hands.
1   2   3   4   5

KEY

MOSTLY 1s Life may be rotten right now, but look for ways to trust God.

MOSTLY 2s Even when you're hurting, life can be easier if you focus on the fact that God cares about you.

MOSTLY 3s Not bad, but work on trusting God and seeking help from others.

MOSTLY 4s Okay, but keep believing that God is in control.

MOSTLY 5s You know God cares and that your parents' problems aren't your fault.

THINGS TO DO

- [ ] Tell all the people in your family that you love them today.
- [ ] Find an adult you can trust enough to talk about difficult things in your life.
- [ ] Write down a verse that talks about God's faithfulness, such as 2 Samuel 22:3 or Psalm 5:11. Put it somewhere you will see it each day as a reminder that God cares about you.
- [ ] Ask God to help you stay strong and remain positive when your family situation gets tough.

THINGS TO REMEMBER

If God cares so wonderfully for flowers that are here today and thrown into the fire tomorrow, he will certainly care for you. **LUKE 12:28**

He loves us with unfailing love; the LORD's faithfulness endures forever. Praise the LORD! **PSALM 117:2**

The LORD is a shelter for the oppressed, a refuge in times of trouble. **PSALM 9:9**

My God is my rock, in whom I find protection. He is my shield, the power that saves me, and my place of safety. He is my refuge, my savior, the one who saves me from violence. **2 SAMUEL 22:3**

Let all who take refuge in you rejoice; let them sing joyful praises forever. Spread your protection over them, that all who love your name may be filled with joy. **PSALM 5:11**

God will not permit any troubles to come upon us, unless He has a specific plan by which great blessing can come out of the difficulty.
PETER MARSHALL

Every evening I turn my worries over to God. He's going to be up all night anyway.
MARY C. CROWLEY

Though our feelings come and go, God's love for us does not.
C. S. LEWIS

Losing Someone

JESSICA'S HEART ACHED like it had never ached before . . . not even when her best friend moved away or when her dog died. She didn't think things would ever feel normal again. She just couldn't believe that her grandmother had died. Since Grandma moved in with Jessica's family, she and Jessica had spent many hours together. Grandma had taught her how to cook some of her famous recipes, and she had been teaching her to knit. Jessica loved talking to her grandmother and hearing stories about when Grandma was a little girl and about Mom when she was growing up. The house was going to feel so empty without Grandma's laughter in it.

"Mom, she wasn't even sick. How could she just die?" Jessica was trying to make sense of it.

"Jess, when God decides it's time for someone to leave this earth, it's time. We need to remember that Grandma loved Jesus and that she's in heaven right now. Right this very minute, she's with God. Plus, she's with Grandpa again and all the people she loved who have already gone there. And someday we'll be with her again, when each of us goes to heaven."

Saying good-bye to people you love is never easy. Even if you have the promise of seeing them again in heaven someday, life here and now can be lonely without them. But one thing that can help you is to concentrate on the joy that your loved one is experiencing right now by being in heaven.

When someone you love dies, it's okay to feel sad. It's okay to cry and to miss them. Those are normal feelings when you lose someone you love. Remember the story in the Bible when Lazarus died and his sisters, Mary and Martha, were so sad? Jesus even cried because his dear friend had died. Don't feel like you aren't supposed to grieve. It's healthy to let those feelings come and to be sad. But after a while, remember heaven and the joy of being together again!

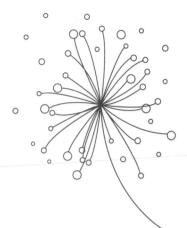

CHECKUP TIME

On a scale of 1 to 5, how do you deal with losing someone you love ?

1 = never
2 = not very often
3 = sometimes
4 = most of the time
5 = always

I let myself cry and grieve when it's time to say good-bye.
1   2   3   4   5

I believe that someday in heaven I will see my loved ones who knew Jesus.
1   2   3   4   5

When someone I love dies, I concentrate on the good memories I have of that person.
1   2   3   4   5

I thank God for the family and friends he has put in my life.
1   2   3   4   5

I tell other people that God loves them so they can experience heaven too.
1   2   3   4   5

KEY

MOSTLY 1s Saying good-bye is hard, but it's time to let God heal your pain.

MOSTLY 2s Choose just one thing to work on, so you can deal with pain better.

MOSTLY 3s Not too bad, but you can work a little on finding joy in God's plan.

MOSTLY 4s Okay, but keep trusting God and sharing his love with others.

MOSTLY 5s You believe in the hope of heaven!

THINGS TO DO

☐ Think about loved ones you have said good-bye to. Write down a few good memories about each person.

☐ Think about the promise of heaven. What are some of the things about heaven that bring you the most joy?

☐ Who in your life do you need to tell about God's love for them?

☐ Ask God to help you accept his love and care when you face losing someone you love.

THINGS TO REMEMBER

Thank God! He gives us victory over sin and death through our Lord Jesus Christ. **1 CORINTHIANS 15:57**

I am the living one. I died, but look— I am alive forever and ever! And I hold the keys of death and the grave. **REVELATION 1:18**

We put our hope in the LORD. He is our help and our shield. **PSALM 33:20**

Since we believe that Jesus died and was raised to life again, we also believe that when Jesus returns, God will bring back with him the believers who have died. **1 THESSALONIANS 4:14**

All praise to God, the Father of our Lord Jesus Christ. It is by his great mercy that we have been born again, because God raised Jesus Christ from the dead. Now we live with great expectation, and we have a priceless inheritance—an inheritance that is kept in heaven for you, pure and undefiled, beyond the reach of change and decay.
1 PETER 1:3-4

Death ends a life, not a relationship.
ROBERT BENCHLEY

Don't cry because it's over. Smile because it happened.
DR. SEUSS

Grief shared is grief diminished.
UNKNOWN

Just Say Thank You

Be thankful in all circumstances, for this is God's will for you who belong to Christ Jesus.
1 THESSALONIANS 5:18

"GRACE, THIS ONE is for you," Mom said as she slid an envelope across the table. Grace opened the card and read these words: "Dear Grace, thank you so much for helping out with my kids last week. I didn't know how it was going to work out for me to work that afternoon when my kids were out of school. You may not realize it, but you were an answer to prayer. I really appreciate you. Love, Mrs. Smith."

Grace was blown away that Mrs. Smith had taken the time to write a card to her. She had thanked Grace over and over for babysitting Friday afternoon when it really was no big deal for Grace. She liked Mrs. Smith's two little kids and enjoyed playing with them.

Grace figured that as a single parent, Mrs. Smith often needed help. But this was the first time Grace had ever offered to babysit before . . . for free! She hadn't realized how much of a help that would be for their family, but Mrs. Smith's gratefulness sure showed her. The card made Grace feel so good that she knew she would look for other chances to help out.

When you do something for someone or help another person in some way, doesn't it feel nice to have that person acknowledge your effort by saying a simple thank-you? Yeah, it's nice to have your gift of time or effort acknowledged in that way. So when people go out of their way to help you or to do something nice for you, give them the gift of your thanks. It's the right thing to do.

And here's another reminder: don't forget to say thanks to God for the many gifts he showers on you every day. Acknowledge the gift of life he has given you, the beautiful world he made for you, the friends and loved ones he has put in your life, his Word . . . well, the list could go on and on. Thank God for all he does, and thank others, too.

CHECKUP TIME

On a scale of 1 to 5, how thankful are you?

1 = never
2 = not very often
3 = sometimes
4 = most of the time
5 = always

I say thank you willingly.
1   2   3   4   5

I write notes of appreciation when someone has done something nice for me.
1   2   3   4   5

I have a grateful heart and attitude.
1   2   3   4   5

I thank God for all he does for me.
1   2   3   4   5

I am quick to notice when people have gone out of their way to help me out.
1   2   3   4   5

KEY

MOSTLY 1s You need to work on thankfulness. Choose one area from the quiz to concentrate on.

MOSTLY 2s You're not very grateful. Keep working on your attitude.

MOSTLY 3s Average—you know you can do better.

MOSTLY 4s Pretty good, but there's a little room for improvement.

MOSTLY 5s Congratulations on your thankful heart.

THINGS TO DO

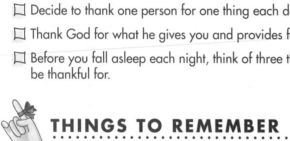

☐ Make a list of people who do things for you each day, and then add some of the things each person does. Don't forget the things we often take for granted, like providing meals and a home to live in.

☐ Decide to thank one person for one thing each day.

☐ Thank God for what he gives you and provides for you.

☐ Before you fall asleep each night, think of three things you can be thankful for.

THINGS TO REMEMBER

Let your roots grow down into him, and let your lives be built on him. Then your faith will grow strong in the truth you were taught, and you will overflow with thankfulness. **COLOSSIANS 2:7**

All of your works will thank you, LORD, and your faithful followers will praise you. **PSALM 145:10**

Don't worry about anything; instead, pray about everything. Tell God what you need, and thank him for all he has done. **PHILIPPIANS 4:6**

Let us come to him with thanksgiving. Let us sing psalms of praise to him. **PSALM 95:2**

Devote yourselves to prayer with an alert mind and a thankful heart. **COLOSSIANS 4:2**

Gratitude is the heart's memory.
FRENCH PROVERB

Thanksgiving is the language of heaven, and we had better start to learn it if we are not to be mere dumb aliens there.
A. J. GOSSIP

Silent gratitude isn't much use to anyone.
GLADYS BRONWYN STERN

Dream Big

KAYLIE THOUGHT LONG and hard about the question staring at her from her homework paper. Her assignment was to imagine what her life will be like fifteen years from now. Kaylie didn't take this lightly. She did have a dream, but she didn't know if she wanted to write it down for her teacher and her classmates to read. She knew it was kind of "out there," but isn't that what dreams are supposed to be? Still, it made her nervous that someone might make fun of her.

Finally, she wrote it down, just to see how it would feel: "I love music. I'm happiest when I'm singing. I think God has given me the ability to sing, and it makes me feel good when I can make other people happy by singing. So my dream is that in fifteen years I will be a professional singer. I want to write and perform worship music, so I can praise God." There, it was done. She stared at the words for a long time and decided to leave them. She had a dream—why not let people know?

Dreams are wonderful! Having a dream of what you'd like to do someday helps you set goals and move in that direction. It is awesome when you start to recognize the abilities and talents God has given you and you can see ways to use them to do his work.

Some people may shoot down your dream (like Kaylie was afraid might happen), but maybe that's just because they don't have dreams themselves or because they just let their dreams pass by. It's wise to see if there's anything you can learn from people's advice or cautions, but don't let them discourage you. Follow your dream until God points you in a different direction. He may lead you through several phases, and you may eventually end up in a different place than where you expected, but someday you will be able to look back and see how that initial dream got you moving to take you where God wanted you to be.

CHECKUP TIME

On a scale of 1 to 5, how good are you at dreaming?

1 = never
2 = not very often
3 = sometimes
4 = most of the time
5 = always

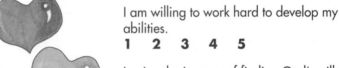

I have a dream for my future.
1   2   3   4   5

I'm using the gifts and talents God gave me.
1   2   3   4   5

I hold on to my dreams, even if other people try to discourage me.
1   2   3   4   5

I am willing to work hard to develop my abilities.
1   2   3   4   5

I enjoy the journey of finding God's will for my life.
1   2   3   4   5

KEY

MOSTLY 1s Come on, you must have a dream. Let your mind explore the possibilities.

MOSTLY 2s Don't be afraid of what others think. Be courageous.

MOSTLY 3s Think outside the box. What would you love to do?

MOSTLY 4s Not bad—maybe you just need a little more courage.

MOSTLY 5s Great job. Dream big and accomplish great things!

THINGS TO DO

- ☐ Make a list of the abilities God has given you.
- ☐ Write down some of your dreams for the next year and for fifteen years from now. Be courageous.
- ☐ Think about people who would encourage you to follow your dream, and share your dream with those people.
- ☐ Ask God for courage to move forward.

THINGS TO REMEMBER

For God's gifts and his call can never be withdrawn. **ROMANS 11:29**

My future is in your hands. **PSALM 31:15**

We can make our plans, but the LORD determines our steps. **PROVERBS 16:9**

"There is hope for your future," says the LORD. **JEREMIAH 31:17**

Never be lazy, but work hard and serve the Lord enthusiastically. **ROMANS 12:11**

When it comes to the future, there are three kinds of people: those who let it happen, those who make it happen, and those who wonder what happened.
JOHN M. RICHARDSON JR.

May the dreams of your past be the reality of your future.
UNKNOWN

I like the dreams of the future better than the history of the past.
THOMAS JEFFERSON

Dark Days

REAGAN SAT QUIETLY at the dinner table. She tried not to make any noise or movements that would draw attention to herself. It would not be a good thing if Dad noticed her. He had been drinking ever since he got home from work, and he was pretty much drunk now. And when Dad had been drinking, he was mean. Mean enough that Reagan was scared of him. She just wanted to get through dinner so she could go up to her room. Then she might be safe.

When Dad was drinking, the slightest thing would make him angry and he'd lose his temper and even start throwing things. When he got that upset, he yelled at her and said it was her fault for doing one thing or another. Reagan felt like such a loser around him. She had a while to go until she turned eighteen, but she already couldn't wait to finish school and leave home.

What an awful situation. No one should have to live that way, but unfortunately lots of people do. The first thing to understand is that alcoholism is a disease. Reagan's dad doesn't get up every morning and decide, *I'm going to make my family miserable today.* He needs help to deal with his addiction and start the process of recovery. The second thing Reagan needs to know is that she is *not* responsible for her dad's behavior. Not on any level.

And when Reagan feels alone, she can remember that there is someone who cares a lot about what her life is like. God cares. Reagan is so important to him—and so are you. God's best plan for you is that you will be cared for, protected, taught, and loved. If that isn't happening in the best way, it doesn't mean he doesn't love you. He loves you more than any person ever could, and he has placed around you people who can help protect you—pastors, neighbors, family members, friends. Remember, God loves you . . . no matter what.

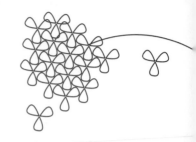

CHECKUP TIME

On a scale of 1 to 5, how are you doing at having hope for the future?

1 = never
2 = not very often
3 = sometimes
4 = most of the time
5 = always

When things are tough, I remember God loves me.

1   2   3   4   5

There is an adult I can trust and talk with.

1   2   3   4   5

I stand strong in the face of fear and discouragement.

1   2   3   4   5

I believe God will care for and protect me.

1   2   3   4   5

I have hope that God has good plans for my future.

1   2   3   4   5

KEY

MOSTLY 1s Life is tough, but you need to work on finding hope.

MOSTLY 2s Choose one thing to do to give you hope for the future.

MOSTLY 3s You have an average hope for the future.

MOSTLY 4s Not bad, but can you trust God more?

MOSTLY 5s Good job! You know God can handle whatever happens in your life.

THINGS TO DO

☐ Make a list of adults you can talk with when things get tough.

☐ If you have a friend who is going through a difficult time with her family, ask if you can pray for her.

☐ Memorize a verse about placing your hope in God, such as Psalm 23:1 or Isaiah 49:23.

☐ Thank God for how much he loves you!

THINGS TO REMEMBER

May integrity and honesty protect me, for I put my hope in you. **PSALM 25:21**

The LORD is my shepherd; I have all that I need. **PSALM 23:1**

But as for me, I will sing about your power. Each morning I will sing with joy about your unfailing love. For you have been my refuge, a place of safety when I am in distress. **PSALM 59:16**

This same God who takes care of me will supply all your needs from his glorious riches, which have been given to us in Christ Jesus. **PHILIPPIANS 4:19**

Those who trust in me will never be put to shame. **ISAIAH 49:23**

You may never know that Jesus is all you need, until Jesus is all you have.
CORRIE TEN BOOM

Where hope grows, miracles blossom.
ELNA RAE

No matter how steep the mountain—the Lord is going to climb it with you.
HELEN STEINER RICE

I Want It All

ZOE HAS A PROBLEM. Well, to be fair, she doesn't think she has a problem, but everyone else does. Here's the deal: Zoe never has enough of anything. If she gets five new pairs of shoes, she wants ten. If someone gives her three sets of earrings, she wants six. If she goes shopping and gets ten shirts, she wants ten more. You get the idea.

Zoe is greedy, and what's worse, she absolutely does not want to share her things with anyone else. If Zoe heard about a girl who had no shoes, it would never occur to her to give that girl some of her shoes . . . even though she has so many she would never miss a pair or two. Zoe wants to have more stuff than anybody else. She wants to have the most—and the best—of everything.

Zoe's attitude is not very attractive, is it? Greedy people do not make good friends, because they can't celebrate with you when something good happens in your life. They aren't able to be happy for you when you get something new because they want whatever you got for themselves. Greedy people can't seem to think about anyone except themselves. They have "I-trouble."

Why is greed such a big deal? It's selfish and self-centered. Greed prevents you from having concern for others and caring about their needs. Try putting yourself in the shoes of a person who has very little. How would you feel if a person who has a lot won't share it with those who need it? Or how would you feel if you got something new but your greedy friend was jealous instead of celebrating with you?

Greed goes against all the guidelines the Bible teaches about how people should relate to one another. Jesus gave a whole message about caring for the poor and needy, even emphasizing how important it is to give a drink of water to a thirsty person. Everything Jesus taught about living in this world encourages loving others and taking care of them by sharing what we have. He even said that when we share with or help another person we are actually showing love to him. Good reason to dump the greedies, huh?

CHECKUP TIME

On a scale of 1 to 5, how greedy are you?

I am able to be content with only what I need.
1   2   3   4   5

1 = never
2 = not very often
3 = sometimes
4 = most of the time
5 = always

I enjoy sharing my stuff with others.
1   2   3   4   5

I'm happy for my friends when they get new things.
1   2   3   4   5

I believe that sharing with others is a way to show my love for God.
1   2   3   4   5

I notice the needs of other people.
1   2   3   4   5

KEY

MOSTLY 1s You have a serious case of the greedies. Find one area to begin working on.

MOSTLY 2s Not good. Look around you—do you see anyone who needs something?

MOSTLY 3s You have an average awareness of those around you.

MOSTLY 4s Not bad, but you have a little room to grow.

MOSTLY 5s Congratulations! You are generous and not controlled by greed.

THINGS TO DO

☐ Think about people who may need basic things like clothes and food. Brainstorm ways you can help them.

☐ Along with a group of friends, organize a food or clothing drive at your church or school.

☐ Go through your closet and figure out what you have a lot of that you could share with someone else. Fill up a bag and take it to an outreach center.

☐ Ask God to soften your heart and make you willing to share.

THINGS TO REMEMBER

Beware! Guard against every kind of greed. Life is not measured by how much you own. **LUKE 12:15**

Let there be no sexual immorality, impurity, or greed among you. Such sins have no place among God's people. **EPHESIANS 5:3**

Share your food with the hungry, and give shelter to the homeless. Give clothes to those who need them, and do not hide from relatives who need your help. **ISAIAH 58:7**

If you have two shirts, give one to the poor. If you have food, share it with those who are hungry. **LUKE 3:11**

All the believers were united in heart and mind. And they felt that what they owned was not their own, so they shared everything they had. **ACTS 4:32**

We tend to forget that happiness doesn't come as a result of getting something we don't have, but rather of recognizing and appreciating what we do have.
FREDERICK KOENIG

He who is greedy is always in want.
HORACE

Greed is a fat demon with a small mouth and whatever you feed it is never enough.
JANWILLEM VAN DE WETERING

Noodle Backbone

ANNA SAT DOWN at the lunch table with her friends and opened her lunch bag. A girl named Cami was sitting a few seats down from Anna and her friends. Cami was new to the school, and Anna had never really talked to her because Anna's friends thought Cami was a total loser.

"Hey look," one of Anna's friends whispered loudly, "Cami the Great is eating pizza!"

"Yeah," another girl said right out loud, "just what her size-eighteen body needs!" Everybody laughed, even Anna (although she didn't really want to).

Cami heard their comments, of course. She put her pizza back on the tray and hung her head. She didn't look up for the rest of the lunch period and didn't eat a bite of anything. Anna felt bad that her friends were picking on Cami. And they did it all day—bumping into her in the hall so she dropped her books, making fun of her clothes, and laughing at her in gym class. Cami didn't have a friend in the whole school. Anna wanted to stand up to her friends and ask them to get to know Cami and give her a chance . . . but she was scared. What if her friends turned on her? What if they made fun of *her*, too? Anna didn't think she was strong enough to take that kind of treatment.

Where can you find the strength necessary to take a stand when you need to? From God! He promises that his incredible strength is available to you. Think about that—God's strength, which made the world, controls the ocean waves, and pushes flowers up through the soil, can help you resist the temptation to mistreat someone just because your friends are doing it. God's strength, which is outlined in story after story in the Bible, will help you with whatever you need to do. So just because you have a certain fear, it doesn't mean you have to fail. God's strength can overcome your own weakness. All you have to do is ask him to help you and be willing to follow wherever he directs and guides you. He'll give you the backbone you need.

CHECKUP TIME

On a scale of 1 to 5, how strong are you?

1 = never
2 = not very often
3 = sometimes
4 = most of the time
5 = always

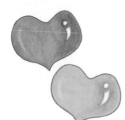

When I make up my mind to do something, I stick to it.
1   2   3   4   5

I ask God to forgive me when I fail to stand up for what's right.
1   2   3   4   5

I am confident about the things I believe.
1   2   3   4   5

I know God will help me be strong.
1   2   3   4   5

I ask God for help in areas where I struggle.
1   2   3   4   5

KEY

MOSTLY 1s Okay, you have the strength of a wet noodle. Choose one area where you need to be stronger, and work on that.

MOSTLY 2s You can do a lot better. Time to toughen up!

MOSTLY 3s You have an average amount of backbone.

MOSTLY 4s Not bad, but you can improve.

MOSTLY 5s Great job! You are one strong girl!

THINGS TO DO

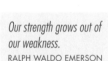

- ☐ Make a list of areas in your life where you need to be stronger. Set a specific goal for each one.

- ☐ Tell a friend about your goals, and ask her to help you stick to them.

- ☐ Write down a verse about God's strength, such as Psalm 23:3 or Isaiah 33:2. Put it on your mirror or dresser or somewhere else you will see it each morning.

- ☐ Ask God to be your strength every day.

THINGS TO REMEMBER

O LORD, do not stay far away! You are my strength; come quickly to my aid!
PSALM 22:19

He renews my strength. He guides me along right paths, bringing honor to his name. **PSALM 23:3**

So think clearly and exercise self-control.
1 PETER 1:13

I also pray that you will understand the incredible greatness of God's power for us who believe him. This is the same mighty power that raised Christ from the dead and seated him in the place of honor at God's right hand in the heavenly realms.
EPHESIANS 1:19-20

LORD, be merciful to us, for we have waited for you. Be our strong arm each day and our salvation in times of trouble. **ISAIAH 33:2**

Our strength grows out of our weakness.
RALPH WALDO EMERSON

If God sends us on strong paths, we are provided strong shoes.
CORRIE TEN BOOM

Perhaps I am stronger than I think.
THOMAS MERTON

Nitpicking Queen

HEIDI IS THE QUEEN . . . the nitpicking queen, that is. She picks her friends apart about silly things, like what they wear, who they talk to at school, who they sit with at lunch, and even what they say in class. It's amazing that Heidi still has friends. For some reason, she seems to thrive on conflict. She acts happiest when someone is arguing with her or cowering in fear when she is attacking them.

Do you have any friends who seem to enjoy arguing? It's not fun, is it? It takes a lot of energy to deal with people like that. Someone who is constantly picking on you makes you feel like you can never live up to her expectations. You are never good enough.

Why do people like Heidi seem to enjoy creating conflict? One reason might be that it makes them feel better about themselves. If they are tearing other people down and making them feel bad, then they think they look better. So they push other people down, then stand on top of them.

Conflict is a miserable way to live. And it's certainly not biblical. God wants people to live together in love, and picking on others shows no love at all. The Bible says that when God's children live in love, it sets us apart from the rest of the world. It shows that we belong to him because we are reflecting his love.

How do you handle someone who constantly

raises conflict? You can refuse to argue with her—just turn and walk away. That helps defuse the conflict. Also, don't believe the negative things she says about you or other people. Concentrate on the positive things about the way God has made you.

CHECKUP TIME

On a scale of 1 to 5, how do you handle conflict?

1 = never
2 = not very often
3 = sometimes
4 = most of the time
5 = always

When someone picks on me, I am able to fight off the negative feelings.

1   2   3   4   5

I can walk away from someone who is trying to raise conflict with me.

1   2   3   4   5

I believe God made me just the way he wants me to be.

1   2   3   4   5

I turn the conversation in a more positive direction when someone is being nitpicky.

1   2   3   4   5

I choose friends who build others up instead of constantly starting fights.

1   2   3   4   5

KEY

MOSTLY 1s You have been giving in to conflict. Choose one area to work on to stand stronger against nitpicking and fighting.

MOSTLY 2s You can do a lot better. Commit to finding more positive ways to handle conflict.

MOSTLY 3s Middle of the road. Try to stand stronger.

MOSTLY 4s Not bad, but you can improve.

MOSTLY 5s Great job! You're standing strong against conflict.

THINGS TO DO

- ☐ Throughout the course of one day, write down all the times you make nitpicky or argumentative comments. What can you do to avoid this?

- ☐ Think about whether you have any friends who are conflict raisers. Consider whether you need to get some new friends.

- ☐ Make a list of things you're grateful for about the way God made you.

- ☐ Ask God to help you focus on the positive and not believe the lies of nitpicking friends.

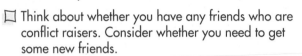

THINGS TO REMEMBER

Better a dry crust eaten in peace than a house filled with feasting—and conflict.
PROVERBS 17:1

Don't speak evil against each other, dear brothers and sisters. If you criticize and judge each other, then you are criticizing and judging God's law. **JAMES 4:11**

For God is not a God of disorder but of peace, as in all the meetings of God's holy people.
1 CORINTHIANS 14:33

Dear brothers and sisters, I close my letter with these last words: Be joyful. Grow to maturity. Encourage each other. Live in harmony and peace. Then the God of love and peace will be with you.
2 CORINTHIANS 13:11

May God our Father and the Lord Jesus Christ give you grace and peace. **EPHESIANS 1:2**

When we judge or criticize another person, it says nothing about that person; it merely says something about our own need to be critical.
RICHARD CARLSON

Any fool can criticize, condemn, and complain but it takes character and self control to be understanding and forgiving.
DALE CARNEGIE

One mustn't criticize other people on grounds where he can't stand perpendicular himself.
MARK TWAIN

No One to Trust

"LYNN, TELL ME what's going on," begged Sheri. "I can tell something is really wrong. Is it something at home? with friends? at school?" Sheri kept asking questions, but Lynn just sat on the floor with tears streaming down her face. She couldn't say a word.

Finally Lynn slowly looked up and said, "I can't tell you. I can't tell anyone." All Lynn's friends knew that something was going on. She hadn't been herself for a couple of weeks. But she wouldn't talk with any of them. She just didn't trust anyone enough to talk about what was going on. Lynn felt like her problem was so serious that her friends would judge her if they knew. She thought no one could help her. She felt completely alone.

It's a terrible feeling to think there is no one you can trust. Some people, like Lynn, are afraid to trust because they think they will be condemned or judged for their actions or feelings. But when they hide things from people, they are actually condemning themselves. They are not giving their friends and family a chance to support and encourage them. Lynn is cutting herself off from support, encouragement, and help. She's trying to make it on her own. But we weren't meant to do life on our own.

To find a person you can trust, you have to be willing to be vulnerable. You have to take a risk and give another person a chance to show you that she can be trusted. Yeah, it's scary, and you shouldn't trust just anybody with the important things in your life. But if you ask God to guide you to the right people and pay attention to who he brings into your life, you will find people you can trust who will give you advice and guidance in line with God's Word and God's love.

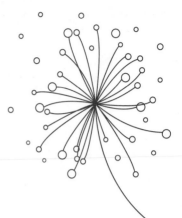

CHECKUP TIME

On a scale of 1 to 5, how trusting are you?

1 = never
2 = not very often
3 = sometimes
4 = most of the time
5 = always

I have people I can trust with my deepest secrets.
1   2   3   4   5

I know I'm not alone because God is always with me.
1   2   3   4   5

I allow others to support and care about me.
1   2   3   4   5

I try to be a friend others can trust.
1   2   3   4   5

I believe God created us to support each other.
1   2   3   4   5

KEY

MOSTLY 1s Don't be so alone. Begin looking for someone you can trust.

MOSTLY 2s Ask God to show you a person worthy of your trust.

MOSTLY 3s You can be more open to allowing others into your life.

MOSTLY 4s You recognize your need for support, but you can do better.

MOSTLY 5s Great job! You trust others and can be trusted yourself.

THINGS TO DO

- ☐ Write down the qualities that make someone trustworthy.

- ☐ Make a list of people you trust enough to talk with about anything. If no one comes to mind, make a list of people you would like to try to trust.

- ☐ Ask your friends if you are someone they can go to with their problems.

- ☐ Ask God to direct you to friends you can be vulnerable with and allow into your life.

THINGS TO REMEMBER

Share each other's burdens, and in this way obey the law of Christ.
GALATIANS 6:2

So encourage each other and build each other up, just as you are already doing.
1 THESSALONIANS 5:11

Love each other with genuine affection, and take delight in honoring each other. **ROMANS 12:10**

Dear friends, let us continue to love one another, for love comes from God. Anyone who loves is a child of God and knows God. **1 JOHN 4:7**

Love means doing what God has commanded us, and he has commanded us to love one another, just as you heard from the beginning. **2 JOHN 1:6**

One must be fond of people and trust them if one is not to make a mess of life.
E. M. FORSTER

To be trusted is a greater compliment than being loved.
GEORGE MACDONALD

You must trust and believe in people or life becomes impossible.
ANTON CHEKHOV

On the Outside Looking In

JILLIAN WATCHED LUCY and her group of friends laughing and talking. It looked like they were having so much fun together. They were always laughing, sharing secrets, and just hanging out. Jillian would have given her right arm to be part of that group. She spent a lot of time watching them and wishing they would notice her. But Lucy and her friends were a closed group. They thought they only needed each other, and they didn't notice anyone who wasn't a part of their little group. Day after day, Jillian sat by herself, but they paid no attention.

Cliques can be tough to break into. Girls who belong to their own exclusive group tend to think alike and enjoy the same things. While it's normal to want to spend time with people who are like you, the trouble comes when anyone else gets shut out. People who are in a clique are often very critical of girls who aren't part of their group. They become so inward focused that they start ignoring other people. It's okay to have a group of friends, but a healthy group is open to new people and welcomes girls who are alone and lonely. After all, God encourages us to love one another. That means including new people in your group and even seeking out those who might be feeling left out.

Doesn't it feel crummy to be on the outside looking in? If you've ever been there, you know it's a lonely feeling. It can make your self-image sink pretty low and make you feel rejected and unloved. If your group of friends acts like a clique, it takes just one person to change things. Be the one to look around and see if there are girls who are alone and need support and encouragement. Be the doorway of your group, and invite others in. You can make a difference.

CHECKUP TIME

On a scale of 1 to 5, how friendly are you?

I invite new people to join what my friends and I are doing.
1   2   3   4   5

1 = never
2 = not very often
3 = sometimes
4 = most of the time
5 = always

I am open to new friends joining my group.
1   2   3   4   5

I notice people who don't seem to have many friends.
1   2   3   4   5

I encourage my friends to be open to others.
1   2   3   4   5

I am kind to people, even if they're not part of my group.
1   2   3   4   5

KEY

MOSTLY 1s Not good. Choose one way you can be more open to people.

MOSTLY 2s How can you and your friends reach out to others?

MOSTLY 3s You can work harder at meeting new people.

MOSTLY 4s Not bad, but you can do better.

MOSTLY 5s Congratulations! You're friendly and considerate of others.

THINGS TO DO

- ☐ Encourage your group of friends to reach out to those who aren't part of your group.

- ☐ Invite one new person to sit at your lunch table this week.

- ☐ Look around for those who are alone or lonely. Think of a way you can reach out to one of those people.

- ☐ Ask God to give you an awareness of those around you who need encouragement and support.

THINGS TO REMEMBER

The purpose of my instruction is that all believers would be filled with love that comes from a pure heart, a clear conscience, and genuine faith. **1 TIMOTHY 1:5**

We have heard of your faith in Christ Jesus and your love for all of God's people. **COLOSSIANS 1:4**

May the Lord make your love for one another and for all people grow and overflow, just as our love for you overflows. **1 THESSALONIANS 3:12**

Dear brothers and sisters, we can't help but thank God for you, because your faith is flourishing and your love for one another is growing. **2 THESSALONIANS 1:3**

What good is it, dear brothers and sisters, if you say you have faith but don't show it by your actions? Can that kind of faith save anyone? **JAMES 2:14**

Wherever there is a human being, there is an opportunity for a kindness.
SENECA

Be kind, for everyone you meet is fighting a hard battle.
PLATO

Kindness is more than deeds. It is an attitude, an expression, a look, a touch. It is anything that lifts another person.
C. NEIL STRAIT

Acknowledgments

A WRITER'S LIFE can be lonely as she sits with her computer. But no book project is a one-person effort. So please allow me to thank a few people for their help:

Thanks to Jerry Watkins, who gave me my first writing opportunity and continues to encourage my efforts.

Thanks to Leah Sutherland for your wonderful illustrations, which help to clearly portray the point of these devotionals.

Thanks to Stephanie Voiland for your expertise in editing and for your patience in working through this project. It's been fun to work together to make this the most usable book possible for the girls who read it.

Thanks to all the wonderful people at Tyndale House Publishers. I appreciate your efforts to print the best products possible that will move people forward in their faith walks.

Straight from the streets of London and hot off the presses of the high school newspaper comes the new series London Confidential. Join fifteen-year-old Savvy and her family as they adjust to the British way of life after moving from the States. Experience the high-fashion world of London and learn about life in England—all while journeying with an all-American girl and budding journalist.

Along the way, you'll probably learn the same lessons Savvy does: it's better to just be yourself, secrets can be complicated, and popularity comes with a high price tag!

Book #1: *Asking for Trouble* (available spring 2010)
Book #2: *Through Thick & Thin* (available spring 2010)
Book #3: The title is still under wraps! (available fall 2010)
Book #4: The title is still under wraps! (available fall 2010)

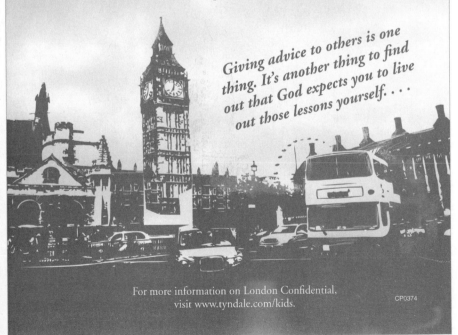

Giving advice to others is one thing. It's another thing to find out that God expects you to live out those lessons yourself. . . .

For more information on London Confidential,
visit www.tyndale.com/kids.

CP0374

Anderson County Library
300 North McDuffie Street
Anderson, South Carolina 29621
(864) 260-4500

Belton, Honea Path, Iva,
Lander Regional, Pendleton,
Piedmont, Powdersville,
Westside, Bookmobile

Jeffrey Brantley, MD
Wendy Millstine, NC

five
good
minutes

with the
one you

love

100 mindful practices to deepen
& renew your love every day

New Harbinger Publications, Inc.

Publisher's Note

Distributed in Canada by Raincoast Books

Copyright © 2007 by Jeffrey Brantley and Wendy Millstine
New Harbinger Publications, Inc.
5674 Shattuck Avenue
Oakland, CA 94609
www.newharbinger.com

Cover design by Amy Shoup; text design by Amy Shoup and Michele Waters-Kermes; acquired by Tesilya Hanauer; edited by Carole Honeychurch

All Rights Reserved. Printed in the United States of America.

Fourth in the Five Good Minutes™ series

Five Good Minutes is a trademark of New Harbinger Publications, Inc.

Library of Congress Cataloging-in-Publication Data

Brantley, Jeffrey.

Five good minutes with the one you love : 100 mindful practices to deepen and renew your love everyday / Jeffrey Brantley and Wendy Millstine.

    p. cm.

  ISBN-13: 978-1-57224-512-9 (pbk. : alk. paper)

  ISBN-10: 1-57224-512-3 (pbk. : alk. paper)

  1. Love. 2. Intimacy (Psychology) 3. Interpersonal communication. 4. Interpersonal relations. I. Matik, Wendy-O, 1966- II. Title.

BF575.L8B7234 2008

158.2--dc22

2007044737

09   08   07

10   9   8   7   6   5   4   3   2   1   First printing

This book is dedicated to all those who have graced my life with their presence and love, and most especially to my dear wife, Mary. May your blessings be multiplied and benefit many others.

—J.B.

In the beginning, there was just life. And then there was life with the love of my best friend, Adrienne Melanie Droogas, whose heartfelt loyalty and sacred love held no boundaries. She is my greatest teacher and inspiration.

—W.M.

contents

introduction

By Jeffrey Brantley, MD

Would you like to try a new approach to love?

What if your partner (or other loved one) joined you?

Love is such a complex subject, with so many faces. So much has been written and said about it already. What would a new approach be like?

Consider the following:

"I love you." These are words everyone wants to hear, and yet these same words, curiously, come more easily sometimes than others.

What does "I love you" look like "in action?"

How do these words feel inside you—deep inside your body, your heart, and your life?

"I love you." These words change and take on richer meaning when relationships grow over time, as awareness builds on affection, and patience and generosity toward one's beloved emerge in actions, both large and small.

Have you ever wished that you could know love more deeply? Renew love more easily and sweetly? Explore the landscape of relationship with your loved one more completely?

"I love you." Speaking these words to another can point both of you toward something great and mysterious about being human and being alive. Would you like to explore that mystery more intentionally every day of your life?

The answers to these (and other) questions about love in your life might be closer than you think. Finding answers and wisdom about love that is true for you might require only that you pay a closer and more kindhearted attention to yourself and to your loved ones in the moments and spaces of daily living.

What if all it takes to enhance your capacity to love—and to nourish and protect all that is good, beautiful, and healthy in yourself, in those you love, and in the world—begins with paying attention, on purpose, in a kind and nonjudging way, right now, in this moment? In this and our other books, we refer to such a way of

paying attention as "being mindful." The awareness that arises from paying attention in a kind and nonjudging way is called *mindfulness.*

In our three previous books, *Five Good Minutes*, *Five Good Minutes in the Evening*, and *Five Good Minutes at Work*, we offered easy, mindfulness-based practices that can be done in just five minutes of "clock time," and yet hold the potential to be radically transforming.

The power of these practices is that they invite you to step back from the rush and momentum of busyness, inattention, and habit energy (the familiar and often unconscious ways of thinking, feeling, and inhabiting your body) and explore the power of being present (being "mindful"). From that base of presence through mindfulness, you are invited to set a clear intention and then to act wholeheartedly in specific, easy-to-follow practices organized around distinct themes for each book.

Presence, intention, and *wholehearted action*—these are the keys to your five good minutes. They are the vehicle for transforming five minutes

of simple clock time into something radically alive, new, and filled with possibility.

In our earlier books, we focused the practices on themes related to daytime activity, evening hours, and work situations. We invited readers to be curious, to have fun, and to explore the possibilities that arise from acting consciously, with intention, in the present moment. The practices we offered ranged from whimsical to reflective to physically engaging.

In this book, we invite you to explore the power of presence, intention, and wholeheartedness through five-minute practices directed at your most important relationships—explicitly, toward those you love. You may want to invite your partner and other loved ones to share some of these practices with you. Any of them can be done by anyone, and a number of them are designed to be shared.

Applied to important relationships, the five-good-minutes approach offers even the busiest people a precious opportunity for

personal enrichment, a wiser relationship to their inner life, and a stronger bond with those they love.

The organizing themes for this book are: "Opening Your Heart," which is about growing self-awareness, warmheartedness, and compassion; "Wise Love," which deals with practices for nourishing, enriching, and protecting your relationship; "Love in Action," which is about facing everyday difficulties and challenges and building the practical skills needed in healthy relationships; and finally, "Cherishing Life."

The final theme, "Cherishing Life," acknowledges that one is continually in relationship to all things, and that by noticing and gently exploring this broader context for love, the depth of feeling for any single person or creature actually grows.

And, if being present, setting intention, and acting wholeheartedly sound either confusing or overly simplistic, don't worry! You will receive very clear instructions, and you can move at your own

pace. Your discoveries and lessons will arise as you actually do the practices.

The five-good-minutes approach is most effective because of what *you* do and *your* direct experience.

Your richest benefits will come from the doing—from your direct experience of practicing mindfulness, of setting intention, and of doing your practice wholeheartedly.

This means that you can have some fun. You don't have to do all 100 practices. And you definitely do *not* have to worry about "getting it right." You are in charge! You decide. If you practice with an honest effort, you cannot do anything wrong. You just have to actually *do* your practice, in some fashion, at your own speed.

In the "Foundation" section of this book, you will find clear and easy-to-follow instructions for practicing mindfulness. Refer back to these instructions as often as you need to. You will learn (and perhaps be pleasantly surprised at what it feels like) to breathe mindfully, to listen mindfully, and to bring mindfulness forward in a wide

variety of ways and places in your relationships. As you explore what it means to be mindful, you will also discover the naturalness and ease of being present. Anyone can do it!

In that same section, you will also learn a bit more about setting intentions and acting wholeheartedly. Be curious and playful, and let yourself be filled with wonder as you develop these dimensions of your five good minutes.

Wise ones have often remarked on the stages of love's mysterious journey: how a commitment to loving someone propels you from a focus on meeting selfish needs through the challenges of partnering and facing life with another to arriving at a point of generous and committed service to many. Such movement through the deepest landscapes of the human heart is possible and available to anyone who actively seeks it.

Done five minutes at a time, a few times a day or a week, the practices in this book can help you and those you love find:

- Ways to open and warm your heart

- Experiences of nourishing, protecting, and deepening your feelings of love

- Methods for handling more skillfully the real challenges and stresses in your relationships

- Opportunities to reflect upon and connect with your place in the larger web of life

PART 1

the foundation

Love Happens Only in the Present Moment

Five minutes is just movement on a clock. The practices and activities in this book invite you to dwell in the present moment, which is always here and is timeless.

Love, in its vast array of wonderful and mysterious expressions, reflecting the deepest places in your heart, happens only in the present moment.

Love, in its wild, funny, energetic, and earthy shapes. Love, in its light and airy, wistful and imaginative outlines. Love, in its moments of intimacy, deep caring, and connection. Love, in its wise and constantly attending and compassionate actions. Love, in its most amazed, awestruck, and reverent forms.

Even the memories and dreams, the hopes and fears you have about someone you love are happening here and now (although the events themselves may be in the past or in your imagined future).

Love (and life) is expressed and experienced always and only in the present moment.

The relationships you share with the ones you love, and especially with "that special someone," also happen only in the present moment.

Those same relationships are a constantly changing tide of togetherness and separation. This ebb and flow of joining and parting, with its distinctive inner and outer flavors and tones (joy and excitement, anger and forgiveness, satisfaction and disappointment, and all the rest) is a strong and deep current rippling through the eternal now of your life.

What if you began to pay closer attention, to notice and allow your feelings of love more freedom and space as part of that flow? What if you started to work with the flow of feelings and experiences in your most important, loving relationships with more curiosity and kindness and less fear or control? What would it feel like to explore

and enact more consciously the intention of deepening and renewing love every day?

What if it were easier than you might think to do these things? And more fun?

You could even invite your partner to join you.

Practicing mindfulness could help you and your partner or other loved one. Mindfulness can be your ally in recognizing and working more gracefully with the ebb and flow in your relationships, including the feelings and tones that are part of that flow. Being more mindful of the love in and around you can lead to a deepening and renewal of the most cherished feelings and relationship with another.

What if by working intentionally and directly with the feeling (or absence) of love in your inner and outer life—here, in the present moment—you could find a stronger and more reliable connection to the deepest places in your heart (and, of course, to the one you love)?

And what if, by being more conscious of the love in your life in the ordinary moments of daily living, you might inhabit all the

moments of your life more fully and find greater joy and satisfaction with whomever and whatever is sharing those moments with you?

Why Five Good Minutes with the One You Love?

Do you ever feel as though you are not really there with your loved one, even though you are there physically?

Have you ever behaved in some way toward your loved one that you later regretted?

Have you ever felt confused or distressed by your feelings about your relationship?

Sadly, the hurry and rush of modern times often distracts us from the people and places that are the most dear and life-affirming. The challenges and stresses you face can interfere with the sense of understanding and togetherness so vital in loving relationships. One frequently can feel alone and isolated and wonder how to recover a sense of belonging and connection.

Where could you turn for help? How might things be different?

Even the busiest people can begin to reconnect with the sources of life and love in a relationship if they learn to inhabit the present moment with sensitive and caring attention. Through these 100 simple, mindfulness-based practices for stopping, relaxing, connecting, and staying here, the momentum of hurry and worry becomes less compelling. Something else more precious and sustaining returns. The opportunity for a different experience arises. Exploration of deeper, more positive feelings suddenly seems possible, even easier.

The 100 practices in this book are aimed at helping you be happier, more satisfied, and a better partner in all of your relationships, and especially in the relationship with your most important other. Each practice is different, engaging, and could be enjoyable, surprising, or even challenging.

Nobody says you have to limit yourself to five minutes, and you don't have to do only one practice in an entire day. Just see what starting there might do for you and for your relationships. Let the wisdom you gain guide your way.

Mindfulness, Your Inner Life, and Love

The 100 practices in this book are organized around four central themes. They are: "Opening Your Heart," "Wise Love," "Love in Action," and "Cherishing Life."

Each of these themes is a doorway into the amazing universe of love. The practices in each section are designed so that you can explore, relax, maybe laugh a bit, and perhaps gain some wisdom and understanding of yourself and those you love.

With that in mind, it may help to know a bit more about each of the themes.

The practices in "Opening Your Heart" focus on the experience of making yourself available for a higher quality of love, one that is deeper, kinder, and more continuous.

You probably know what it feels like to put someone out of your heart. How this act can lead to a feeling that your heart is closed and hardened. How hardening the heart can lead to feelings of isolation and separation.

The practices in this first section are aimed at helping you explore wise and skillful means for softening, warming, and opening your heart. You are invited in these practices to make a space inside to let other people and life's experiences back *into* your heart and to feel more ease and joy as you do.

The practices in "Wise Love" invite you to consider the possibility that there is no end to the unfolding of true love in your relationships. While there is a beginning and a middle, perhaps, your capacity for expanding and deepening caring, tenderness, and joy with your loved one literally knows no limits.

Wise love recognizes that in love, one size does not fit all. As people change, relationships also change. Cultivating a shared space of affection, patience, and respect that recognizes and allows for change can support the unfolding of love in ways and directions unsuspected.

The practices in this second section focus on such positive and profound expressions of love as applying stronger attention; showing

affection, kindness, and compassion; and exploring patience, generosity, and laughter together.

The practices in "Love in Action" recognize that love and relationships do not always go smoothly or happily. What can be done with the painful, difficult, and challenging moments and situations?

The greatness of your own heart comes through often most clearly in those times of difficulty and distress. You can learn to notice the difference in your direct experience when there is some level of contraction through fear, aversion, or pain and when there is openness of heart through courage and kind awareness.

The practices in this third section invite you to explore the power of attention, kindness, and compassion in caring for yourself and for another when feelings of upset and stress create friction and apparent separation in your relationship.

The practices in "Cherishing Life" offer you an opportunity to explore a larger landscape of loving relationships. What is happening

in your feelings of connection and affection for those beyond your closest relations?

In this fourth section, you are invited to engage in practices that help you explore directly how love can show itself in the complex web of all the relationships that make up your life.

You could learn more about how love's mysterious journey can take you from self-centeredness to other-awareness and concern, to feelings of connection and compassion for all living things.

The practices in this section offer interesting and imaginative ways to explore your amazing connections to the larger web of life.

How to Use This Book

The 100 practices in this book offer specific opportunities for deepening love and enriching your relationships, and they are organized around the four themes discussed in the previous section: "Opening Your Heart," "Wise Love," "Love in Action," and "Cherishing Life."

You do *not* have to do all 100 practices to benefit from this book.

You do *not* have to like or enjoy all 100 practices to benefit.

You definitely do *not* have to work through the practices in any particular order or sequence, including 1 through 100.

What is helpful is to approach each practice in the spirit of relaxing and having fun. Try not to get caught up in the drama or heaviness often associated with relationships and with love, and instead, relax, letting yourself rest in a spirit of curiosity and experimentation. Allow yourself to be surprised. Letting go of trying to make anything special happen or of any attachment to outcomes will serve you well.

It is important to be patient with yourself. From our point of view, you cannot make a mistake doing any practice as long as you are willing to make an honest effort.

We suggest you read through and work with the practices in any way you like. Look for the ones that appeal to you. When one sounds

like fun, or piques your curiosity, or perhaps evokes a sense of relief and ease inside you, then that could be a good place to begin.

You will likely find it helpful to read through your practice a few times before actually doing it. You may want to ask someone to read it to you. Sharing the practice with another, your loved one, for example, or even a group, can often be quite rewarding.

You will probably recognize over time, as you work with the practices, that what appeals to you can change from day to day. This means it is good to go back and review different and untried practices from time to time. Again, the spirit of exploration, curiosity, and discovery will carry you a long way.

Mindfulness: Your First "Good" Minute

Life and love are happening in the present moment, and the riches they offer are only available when you are present, here and now.

Establishing your attention in the present moment is the first minute of your five good minutes. You will see that many of the

practices in this book begin with "breathe mindfully for about a minute," or "listen mindfully for about a minute," or "bring mindful attention" to a particular bodily sensation for about a minute.

Later in this section, you will find easy-to-follow instructions for mindful breathing, listening, and attention to bodily experience.

Return to these instructions for practicing mindfulness as often as you like. Work with them until they become your friend and refuge. Mindfulness is truly a practice. You "practice" not to become perfect but to learn what it really means to be mindful and to trust that you can actually be mindful no matter how stressful or demanding the conditions of a given moment may be. The benefits you gain from the practices in this book are directly related to your actual practice of mindfulness—not just reading about it!

You may want to consider practicing mindfulness together with your partner or loved one. The rewards that come from sharing just the mindfulness aspect of *Five Good Minutes with the One You Love* might surprise both of you!

Being present includes feeling a sense of ease and calm as you pay attention mindfully. You will probably notice that your mind and body naturally move into a calmer and more peaceful state as you practice mindfulness. But, being mindful does not stop at or require you to be calm. You can actually be mindful and allowing of an intense, even upsetting experience as it happens. Paradoxically, by bringing mindfulness to the upset and difficulty, you can experience a greater inner space surrounding the upset. So, you may not be calm, but you can be more peaceful even as you are feeling upset!

If this all sounds too far-fetched, don't worry. As you actually *practice* mindful breathing, listening, or attention to bodily sensations, you will experience mindfulness directly and understand its true power.

When you are practicing mindfulness, you are actually resting in an awareness that is here and now and is not judging or trying to change anything. In other words, you are dwelling more consciously and deeply in the present moment.

By learning to establish mindfulness and to inhabit the present moment more fully, you learn to "step out" of the momentum of habit energy and busyness that interferes with your most important relationships. That is why practicing mindfulness—being consciously present—is the first "good" minute. It makes you more available for everything else.

Beginning Your Mindfulness Practice

It takes some skill and practice to be truly present. When you pay attention mindfully, you are not trying to add to or subtract anything from the present moment. Being mindful means making enough effort to be present but not trying too hard.

As you develop your mindfulness practice, you will probably find yourself relaxing more and more. You do not have to *do* anything (except learn to pay closer, allowing attention in different situations and moments). You don't have to make anything special happen. Your kind, sensitive, and nonjudging attention is all that is required.

There are many methods to establish mindfulness. They all involve paying attention on purpose in a kind and nonjudging way. You can pay attention to particular things (like breath or sounds or sensations) or you can rest in a broader, more open, nonselecting awareness that receives whatever flows into the present moment.

In this book, we rely on three methods of practicing mindfulness that are especially important. They all start with picking a particular object as the initial focus for your mindful attention. The objects are breath sensations, sounds, and sensations in your body. These methods are mindful breathing, mindful listening, and mindful attention to bodily sensations. Many of the practices begin with the invitation to use one of these mindfulness methods for your first good minute.

Each of these ways of practicing mindfulness is extremely potent and has a long history among those who teach and practice meditation. You may even have heard or read about or practiced one or more of these methods before now. If that is the case—that you are

already familiar and comfortable with mindfulness of breathing, or listening, or of bodily sensations—then feel free to practice as you already know how. On the other hand, if it helps you to refine or sharpen your ability to be mindful, refer to the following instructions as often as you need to.

You may ask: When and why would I choose mindful breathing over mindful listening or mindful attention to bodily sensations?

First, you should know that by picking any of these focal points (or any other specific object) for mindful attention, you effectively establish yourself in the present moment and step outside the flow of identification of and reactivity to the demands of thoughts, feelings, and other experience in the present moment. So, any method of practicing mindfulness depends at least to some extent on establishing attention here and now. By learning to rely on the sensations of your breath or body, or on the sounds happening around you as your objects of mindfulness, you will have some powerful and different methods to connect with the present moment.

For example, many find that it can be difficult to concentrate attention on the breathing when their minds are racing or very busy. Or, they may find that sounds in a noisy situation distract them from mindful attention to breath or bodily sensations. Or, bodily sensations themselves may be urgent and demanding of attention.

Mindful listening in such moments can help you to access a sense of inner spaciousness that can then include all that is happening, including the distractions.

Alternatively, if you are feeling spaced out or out of touch with your body, restless, or agitated, taking a narrow focus of attention on breath sensations or on the sensations flowing through your body can be just the thing to bring you into the present moment with an increased sense of stillness and calm.

By learning methods of being mindful of each of these conditions—breath sensations, sounds, or bodily feelings—you empower yourself to work more skillfully with any challenge that may arise to being mindful, and therefore more present.

You will see as you work with these methods of mindfulness (and others) that being mindful is truly an art.

Sometimes, the art lies in selecting the means of being mindful that fits most naturally into the circumstances of the present moment. For example, if there are loud noises around you, mindful listening may be most natural as a beginning place for mindfulness. Alternatively, if you are engaged in activity that produces strong physical sensations, it can be skillful to focus directly on the feelings flowing through your body.

In any case, your art of mindfulness is also about the attitudes that you bring to each moment. It's important that you remain patient with yourself, and kind, and recognize that your attention will wander. When that happens you have not made a mistake! As you learn to work with being more present and connected in different situations, with varying amounts of distraction and challenges, your art of being present will grow stronger.

Instructions for Mindful Breathing

① Make yourself comfortable. You can do mindful breathing in any posture: sitting, lying down, standing, or even walking.

② To reduce distractions, close your eyes gently. If closing your eyes is uncomfortable, you could leave them open about halfway and gaze with a soft focus at a spot a few feet ahead of you on the ground.

③ For the duration of this practice, you don't have to make anything happen or become anyone else other than who you already are. You already have all you need to be mindful. You can trust that.

④ Gently bring your attention to the place in your body where it is easiest for you to feel the direct sensations of your breath moving in and out. You don't have to control the breath in any way—just pay attention to the sensations as they happen. The tip of the nose, the chest, and the abdomen rising and falling are common places that people rest their attention when practicing mindful breathing.

⑤ Let the direct physical sensations of the moving breath in your body be your object of attention. Notice rising and falling, in and out, deep and shallow, cool and warm, for example. Let the breath sensations come to you. Let them into your awareness. Notice the sensations of in-breath, a pause, of out-breath, and a longer pause. Perhaps notice how each in-breath has a beginning, a middle, and an end. So does each out-breath.

⑥ When your attention wanders or is distracted by something, you have not made a mistake or done anything wrong. Simply notice this movement of your attention, recognize it as a habit of your mind, and kindly let the breath sensations back into your awareness. Let the breath sensations come back to you. Your mind will probably move off the breath sensations countless times as you practice mindful breathing in your life. The movement isn't important. What counts is that you recognize it and how you relate to the fact that your attention moves. Each time, let yourself be kind and patient,

not judging yourself but simply noticing the movement and allowing the breath sensations back in.

⑦ Notice any sense of struggle you may feel and have patience and compassion for yourself and that feeling. It may be impossible at times to focus on more than one breath or on a series of breaths before the attention wanders. That does not have to be a problem. Just focus on *this* breath. Come back to *this* breath. Being attentive and present for *this* breath is good enough.

⑧ End your meditation by shifting your focus off the breath sensations, opening your eyes, and moving gently.

Instructions for Mindful Listening

① Make yourself comfortable. You can do mindful listening in any posture.

② If it helps, let your eyes close gently.

③ For the length of this practice, let go of all agendas and of trying to change anything or to make anything special happen.

④ Softly bring the focus of your attention to the sounds around you. Let them come to you. Let them into your awareness, without choosing one over another, but meeting each one with equal attention and interest.

⑤ Notice and let go of any thoughts or stories or reactions you have to any sound. Focus on the direct experience of the sound, including its tone, loudness, vibration qualities, and how near or far away it is.

⑥ Allow your attention to include all sounds, noticing how they come and go, arising, changing, and fading away. Perhaps you can begin to notice the spaces and silences between and

around the sounds as well. Whatever you notice, allow yourself to relax, soften, and open.

⑦ Let the meditation support you. Let the sounds come to you
and let them go rather than looking for them or clinging
to one instead of another. Notice how one sound fades and
is replaced by another in your awareness. Let yourself rest
inside any sense of increasing stillness and receive all the
sounds from that place.

⑧ End your meditation by shifting your focus off the sounds,
opening your eyes, and moving gently.

Instructions for Mindfulness of Bodily Sensations

①   Make yourself comfortable. You can practice mindfulness of bodily sensations in any posture.

②   If it helps you to focus attention, let your eyes close gently.

③   For the time of this practice, let go of rushing, doing, and trying to make things happen. Relax. You already have what you need to be mindful. The capacity for kind attention in the present moment is already within you.

④   Bring your attention gently to the flow of sensations in your body. Let the direct feelings of heaviness, pressure, or vibration, for example, come into your awareness. Notice feelings of warmth and coolness, dampness and dryness, contractions and sensations of release as they unfold in your body.

⑤   Play with letting go of any thoughts or ideas that come up about your body or its parts. Don't get caught up in the names of the different parts, either. Focus instead on the bare sensations, noticing how they arise, change, and fade.

See how much interest and sensitive attention you can bring to the flow of direct, changing sensations.

⑥ Let your attention penetrate deeply and yet remain light and soft with each sensation. Notice any tendency to grasp onto one sensation or to try to get rid of another one. Let those urges to cling to or reject sensations go, noticing those sensations as just activity in your inner body.

⑦ As in any other mindfulness practice, when your mind wanders, you have not made a mistake. Just notice where it went and return attention to the flow of bodily sensations.

⑧ When you are ready to end your practice, softly open your eyes and move gently.

Intention: The Second Element of Your Five Good Minutes

Setting a clear intention is a way of pointing yourself in the direction of an important value or goal. The practices in *Five Good Minutes with the One You Love* all involve setting and acting on an intention. Many of them invite you to be very explicit about actually speaking your intention (at least to yourself) as your second good minute.

Setting your intention can be done skillfully or unskillfully. That is, you can help yourself move toward your goal with a skillful intention, and you may get in your own way with an unskillful intention.

For example, it would not be skillful to set an intention that you should become completely free of disturbing worries about your loved one from doing a single five-minute practice! It's important that you do not set intentions that are unrealistic or that you must achieve at all costs. That kind of intention is a setup for harsh self-criticism and self-doubt about your ability to do anything to help yourself.

A skillful intention is more like a friendly guide or a good traveling companion. It points you toward places and things you want to visit and helps you get there. It doesn't hurry or criticize or demand but instead acknowledges that important changes can take time. A skillful intention is also infused with patience and kindness.

For example, you may set an intention to be more understanding in your relationship. A skillful intention does not demand instant or dramatic results and does not give up when impatience and frustration return to the relationship. When challenges appear, the skillful intention to be more understanding simply becomes more resolved and curious about moving in the direction of greater understanding.

Acting Wholeheartedly: The Final Piece of Your Five Good Minutes

Acting wholeheartedly means doing something with all of your attention and energy. It means giving it your best effort. If you have already

established presence through mindfulness and have set a clear intention, then you possess a powerful base for wholehearted action.

As you do the specific instructions for the practice you have chosen—reflecting on forgiveness, for example, or laughing out loud with your loved one—acting wholeheartedly means doing it with all your heart and without attachment to outcome. In other words, just do it! Don't let yourself get caught up in watching to see if anything is changing as you do your practice. Relax. Just do it. Then see where you are without spinning more stories about control or making things happen. In the framework of this book, wherever your practice takes you is fine. You will very likely learn something useful, discover something that needs attention, taste something rich, or have some fun along the way.

It is helpful to recall that there is a kind of paradox operating here. Recognizing and working with the paradox is another element in the art of practicing your five good minutes.

The paradox is that you *do* want things to be different, but the more you push and pull, strive and strain to make them that way, the more likely you are to be frustrated! This will be true in doing your five good minutes, and it very likely happens in other corners of your life and relationships as well.

So, in doing your practice, beware of pushing and pulling so hard toward a specific goal or outcome. See if in the doing of your practice you might discover something you had *not* planned or decided *should* happen. See if life might surprise and amaze you—or even teach you a thing or two. Each time you choose and practice a five-good-minutes exercise you have another opportunity to experience acting without attachment to outcome.

Learning to act wholeheartedly can be the open window that allows life to surprise and amaze you again and again. (And that surprise and amazement may just spill over into other corners of your life, too.)

It is also perfectly okay if you feel awkward, silly, or even embarrassed as you do your practice wholeheartedly. Remember, you cannot make a mistake as long as you give it your best effort. Just acknowledge and honor whatever you are feeling as it happens (which is a moment of mindfulness, by the way) and carry on.

So be curious, be patient, be kind and forgiving of yourself. Explore different practices and give yourself some room to learn and to grow.

100 New Approaches to Love

Whatever you do can become something new, fresh, and beautiful when you are truly present and open to the possibilities and marvels that are available here, in the present moment.

In just five good minutes, through mindfulness and presence, skillful intention, and acting wholeheartedly, you can discover exciting new dimensions in your relationships to even the most familiar people and conditions in your life.

As human beings, we share a longing for love and connection, and we have unlimited capacity within our own being to express, give, and receive love.

May the practices in this book support you in growing, renewing, or simply enjoying the loves in your life in ways deeper and richer than you may have ever imagined.

And may these 100 approaches to love—made new and fresh by your cultivating kindness and allowing present-moment attention to actions—promote peace, understanding, and goodwill throughout our world.

PART 2

the practices

opening your heart

open the door for love

At the heart of your desire to be loved is the ability to love yourself, to cherish the good, the not-so-good, and everything else in between. Take this moment to let kind, loving energy shine in on you.

① Make a mental or written list of three physical traits that you love about yourself, such as your smile, hair, and belly.

②   Make a mental or written list of three personality traits that you love about yourself, such as your sense of humor, wit, and intellect.

③   Now make a final list of three ways that you're good at sharing your love, such as a talent for nurturing others, being a good listener, and the ability to be compassionate.

By focusing your attention on being loving to yourself, you allow the doors of self-love to open and the warm light of kindness to shine into your life. ♡

glad to be alive

Do you ever find yourself feeling distressed and not wanting to go forward with your daily schedule?

Let the powerful synergy of kindness, compassion, and appreciation renew and revitalize you.

① When you notice yourself feeling closed down or irritable, stop and acknowledge that.

② Breathe mindfully for about a minute.

③ Set your intention. For example: "May I be free from this contraction and open to joy."

④ Breathe mindfully for a few more breaths.

⑤ To yourself, say the affirmation: "Glad to be alive." Notice your inner life. If you are upset, kindly acknowledge that and add: "Upset *and* glad to be alive."

⑥ If you feel pain or distress, offer yourself compassion. For example: "May I be free from pain and upset."

⑦ Repeat your affirmation, "glad to be alive," gently and quietly several times.

⑧ Notice any thoughts or feelings that come to you. Acknowledge and honor them.

⑨ Remember your sources of joy. ♡

write from the heart

Your frantically paced life may leave you little time to write your feelings. Take this moment to write yourself a love letter. Through writing, you can channel your love inward. Keep this letter with you as a reminder of the endless well of affection you have for yourself. Here are some suggestions for generating that love note:

- List ten things that you love about yourself.

- Start with "Dear [your name]," and imagine someone madly in love with you whispering into your ear. What kind of romantic expressions would he or she say?

- Write about a selfless and caring act that you did for someone.

- Write the following five times: "I love and cherish you inside and out, each and every day."

- Write the following three times: "You are a magnificent and radiant person. There is only love and compassion here for you."

You can even put this letter in the mail to yourself and open it when you need a boost of self-love. ♡

4

make room for love

Have you ever noticed how negative emotions such as anger and resentment can take up enormous space in your life? Well, move over hatred! Let's make room for more love. Take these next few minutes for an expansive love meditation.

① Find a place to be still and relax.

② Ask yourself: "What is the capacity of my heart to love? Just how much love is really in there?"

③ Close your eyes and imagine a swirling groundswell of loving emotions intensifying inside you. You are tapping into your ever-expanding pool of affection and kindness.

④ Pay attention to what you're feeling right now in your body. Imagine this abundant love spilling out from your heart and rapidly spreading throughout your body. What physical sensations are you experiencing? Do you feel warm inside? Do you feel surrounded by good energy?

⑤ Open your eyes and reassure yourself that you have a vast capacity to love. You truly are an unstoppable force of benevolence toward yourself and others. ♡

relaxed body, clear mind, open heart

Stress and tension in your body, coupled with worry and hurry in your mind, can be barriers to an open heart.

Try the following practice for self-care of body and mind, and see what happens in your heart space:

① Select a time and place where you will not be disturbed and breathe or listen mindfully for about a minute.

② Set your intention. For example: "May this practice bring me wisdom."

③ Bring mindful attention to your body. Imagine that each in-breath fills you with ease and each out-breath carries away tension and stress.

④ After a few breaths, bring mindfulness to any thoughts or stories that come up. Let them be. No need to fight them or follow them. Let them go.

⑤ After a few more mindful breaths, bring attention to your heart space. What is happening there now? ♡

6

cultivate curiosity

Studies show that there is a link between curiosity and well-being. In fact, highly curious people report greater satisfaction with life. If you know someone who's obsessed with a hobby, whether it's quilting or car restoration, then you're familiar with how highly motivated he or she can be with a project. What you might not know is that curiosity can be cultivated, even when you're not feeling motivated.

- Begin by working with what you have. Unbury those old treasures stored away that used to inspire you, such as a musical

instrument, arts and crafts projects, or your tennis racket. Schedule a time on your calendar to reconnect with the enjoyment you experienced with these activities.

- When you start a project, don't focus on the outcome or the final product. Instead, pay attention to the process. This exploration isn't a contest or race to the finish line, so just enjoy this moment in your self-discovery.

- Try something new! Invite a friend to participate in pursuing a new interest that seems intimidating, such as painting or martial arts.

- Make a pact with yourself that you're going to follow through on this pursuit and not criticize yourself.

Developing a sense of wonder can bring greater meaning to your life. ♡

silent harmony

Throughout the ages, great spiritual philosophers have encouraged people to align themselves with peace and love. Unfortunately, there is little peace on our planet. Take this meditative moment to be mindful of how cultivating serenity within yourself can attract harmony in the world.

① Quietly and while seated comfortably, take a few deep breaths. On the inhale, take in the calm and serenity that you desire. On the exhale, let go of the turmoil and madness of the world.

② Let the noises of your mind drift off. Let your cluttered thoughts and everyday distractions dissipate. You are safe and free to leave your fears and worries behind.

③ Imagine opening a door within your heart to infinite peace and harmony. Be aware of the power of your inner peace as a magnet for tranquility in the world around you. May it be so. ♡

breathe mindfully

Worries, busyness, pain, and upset are real. They happen to you and can create feelings of isolation and disconnection.

It is important and helpful to recognize when such separation happens and also to recognize that, although these intense energies are yours, they are not you!

Mindful breathing can help you realize and remember that you are more than any challenging energy. It can allow you to rest in a steadier and wider dimension.

① Select a time and place where you will not be disturbed.

② Breathe mindfully for about a minute.

③ Set your intention. For example: "May mindful breathing bring me peace and wisdom."

④ For the rest of this practice, relax and just breathe mindfully.

⑤ Remember that mindful breathing is not a breathing exercise. It is an awareness practice.

⑥ Let sensitivity, kindness, and awareness grow in you as you repeatedly let the breath sensations "back in." ♡

9

---

free your heart

Your past can haunt you and sabotage your ability to feel lovable. Old emotional wounds from past breakups or traumas can be obstacles to remaining open to love. Taking a self-nurturing five minutes to heal old wounds will help you give and receive the loving kindness that you truly desire.

① When you find those painful losses and hurtful emotions stomping around loudly in your life, let them be your signal to be gentle with your heart.

② Acknowledge your past wounds by making a mental or written list of a few hurtful occasions.

③ Go down your list and recite a healing prayer for forgiveness for each and every situation. Say aloud or to yourself: "Through this ritual of forgiveness, I am freeing myself from past wrongs and injuries. I am showering my old heartache with compassion to set me free to give and receive abundant love." ♡

rest in beauty

When you are feeling closed off, isolated, or alone, relief is closer than you might think.

Learn to restore and reconnect by resting in beauty.

Your key to connection lies in mindful attention to the fullness and beauty of life around you.

① Stop whatever you are doing and practice mindful breathing, listening, or movement for about a minute.

②   Set your intention. For example: "May this practice of attention to beauty revitalize me."

③   Continue mindfulness practice for a few more breaths.

④   Look around you. Notice beauty. See it in color, shape, space, motion. When you find something beautiful, look closer. Rest there.

⑤   Listen mindfully. Find the beauty in sounds. Hear the tones, rhythm, and silence.

⑥   Find beauty around you using your other senses—smell, taste, touch.

⑦   Rest in all the beauty around you. ♡

give it away

Love comes to us when we give it away. In fact, the more love you give, the more love you have to give. Right now, take five minutes to share your love. Make the most of it, and be generous! Here are some suggestions to get you started:

- Plan a meal that will be infused with your love.

- Write a love note to someone you care about and copy the same note for yourself.

- Call someone dear to you and tell her how much you love her. Then call yourself and leave a message declaring your love.

- Donate money or clothes to a charity or give a gift or something meaningful to a friend or stranger.

- Practice being generous and patient with your coworkers, customers, the cashier-clerk, and the driver with road rage.

- Be loving with a stranger by offering a smile, saying hello, wishing him a nice day, or giving her a compliment.

- When you make others feel good, it has a magical way of making you feel good. ♡

feel the joy

Great joy resides in the everyday moments of your life.

Opening to and connecting with the happiness already suffusing your life rather than waiting for something exciting or "special" to happen can warm and open your heart immediately.

Learn to let the happiness of others be a doorway to your own happiness.

① When you are around either friends or strangers, pause and collect your attention by breathing mindfully for about a minute.

② Set your intention. For example: "May I recognize and feel the joy around me."

③ Look around. Notice someone who appears happy. Without interrupting him, pay attention to his joy. Let it touch you. Let it bring you a smile.

④ To yourself, quietly wish him continued happiness. You might use the silent phrase, "May your joy never end."

⑤ Breathe mindfully. Rest in the happiness you feel. ♡

soft belly

You can be surrounded by all the love you could ever want, but when your life gets maxed out with stress, frustration, and fatigue, love may not be enough. Take this next five-minute mindful reprieve to slow down your pace and relax into the moment.

① Begin seated in a quiet and comfortable space, if possible.

② Close your eyes and take a few slow breaths, acknowledging and then letting go of any pockets of tension with each exhale.

③ Now focus on softening your belly, releasing any tightened muscles or feelings of anxiety. Let your stomach go limp while allowing your belly to rise and fall with each breath.

④ Worries and stresses may wander in and out of your mind, but keep your attention on your relaxed abdomen.

When love falls short of your expectations, just remember that a soft belly helps maintain a relaxed mind. And when you're feeling calm, love and happiness can find their way back into your life. ♡

your good works

Everyone has experienced feeling stuck in negative self-talk and a sense of failure.

The meanness of criticism you direct at yourself can quickly lead to a closing and hardening of your heart.

See how remembering your own good deeds and works helps to open your heart again.

① When you notice that your heart has become hard or closed, breathe mindfully for about a minute.

② Set your intention. For example: "May this practice warm and soften my heart."

③ Bring mindful attention to your body. Let the body soften and relax with each exhale.

④ Recall something good you did for another. It could be a favor, a gift, a sacrifice, an offering, or some kindness.

⑤ Reflect on the benefits of your good works for that person. Feel her happiness in your body and in your heart.

⑥ Remember and relax into the goodness within you. ♡

blessings to you

Do you have someone in your life whom you find hard to love? Perhaps this person is emotionally shut down or difficult to connect with. Try this blessing prayer. It may surprise you with wonderful and unexpected results.

① Make a mental or written list of three things about that person that you don't like.

② Now make a mental or written list of three things about that person that you do like.

③ After each item listed, say aloud a prayer to bless him for all that is good and all that is complicated with that person. You may want to speak his name aloud, followed by: "For all the difficult parts of you, I bless you. I bless you and wish that only love and joy fills your heart." Follow this with: "For all the gentle and kind parts of you, I bless you. I bless you and wish you abundant happiness every day."

The blessing prayer works best with practice on a daily basis and has astonishing outcomes. ♡

16

silent renewal

Modern life is so full of external distractions, busyness, and interruptions that it is easy to forget one of your most powerful sources of renewal and vitality.

Silence.

Spaces of silence exist over, under, around, and within all the sources of sound and noise in your life—even those sources in your own mind.

Silence is always there, waiting for your attention, waiting to offer you peace and joy.

① Find a comfortable place and breathe mindfully for about a minute.

② Set your intention. For example: "May this practice bring me ease and well-being."

③ Breathe mindfully for a few more breaths.

④ Gently shift your attention to sounds and listen mindfully. Hear all sounds, allowing them in, letting them come and go.

⑤ Focus more closely. Notice the space before and after each sound.

⑥ Relax and rest in the silent spaces. ♡

circle of love

Difficult times in your life create obstacles to opening yourself to love. The following visualization will help you create a beaming circle of love that will radiate inward and outward throughout your day.

Imagine you are lying comfortably in a safe and undisturbed place, such as your bedroom or a peaceful meadow. You are free of worries and constraints, deadlines and demands. You are relaxed and calm. Now visualize a golden light encircling your whole body. The light represents all the love there is in the

world. The light is warm and soothing, comforting and reassuring. The light is like a healing balm to past relationship wounds, to the loss of a loved one, to grief. The light holds the power to calm volatile emotions, such as anger, resentment, and fear. It has the ability to mend broken hearts and repair damaged personal connections.

Take this moment to visualize the healing nature of your love. Do you feel more serene, uplifted, happy? Remind yourself daily that your love circle surrounds you at all times. You simply need to bring it to mind for it to work its healing magic. ♡

deepest desires

As your schedule rapidly fills up, you have less and less time or energy to follow your true passions, such as painting, gardening, or dancing. You may need a refresher on what those deepest desires are and why they're so vital in maintaining your happiness. It's time to unbury them. Take the next few minutes to reprioritize your schedule to make room for the things in your life that bring meaning.

- If you like to do art, make a list of what you need to get the next project started.

- If you enjoy the outdoors, take a brisk walk around your neighborhood.

- If you like to exercise but never have time to get to the gym, drop and do a few minutes of a floor routine for strengthening your abdomen and back muscles. Or, put in that aerobic video, pronto!

- If you want to eat healthily, make a list of ingredients for a nutritious meal tonight.

Your art or true passions are sacred ways to nourish the spirit of love that lives inside of you. ♡

your own best friend

For many reasons, people tend to omit themselves from any list of their best friends.

What would it feel like to add yourself to that list?

Try "befriending" yourself with the following practice:

① Find a place where you can relax without interruption. Breathe mindfully for about a minute.

② Set your intention. For example: "May this practice bring me ease and well-being."

③ Visualize yourself sitting with a close friend. Feel your affection for your friend.

④ Imagine speaking to him or her warmly, wishing him or her well. You might say: "May you be safe and well," or, "May you be happy and healthy."

⑤ Now imagine speaking to yourself with the same feeling. Be as kind to yourself as you are to your friend: "May I be safe and well. May I be happy and healthy."

⑥ Acknowledge and hold with compassion any feelings that arise. ♡

count your blessings

When the judging mind is in session, the heart feels closed, and feelings of anger and upset often prevail.

Shifting your focus from what's wrong to what's right can change everything.

Whenever you are caught churning in judgment, try the following practice:

① Notice your inner world of criticizing and judging. Begin breathing mindfully and continue for about a minute.

② Set your intention. For example: "May this practice reconnect me with ease and joy."

③ Focus more closely on breath sensations as you breathe mindfully for a few more breaths.

④ Shift attention to your body. Breathe mindfully, feeling sensations. Appreciate how your body works to sustain your life.

⑤ Look around you. Acknowledge the helpful people and things that support your present situation.

⑥ Nurture any feelings of gratitude arising in you, and rest there. ♡

activist of the heart

Be a warrior for love! Be aware that everywhere you go, everyone you meet, and every situation that you face can be an opportunity for radical infusions of love. As a love activist, never doubt that you can have a profound effect on your family, friends, neighbors, and community. One small selfless act of loving kindness, such as bringing in an empty garbage can for a neighbor, sending an affectionate card to a friend, or writing a gratitude letter to your partner, can have a

positive ripple effect. Take this mindful moment to wholeheartedly make a declaration to love as many people as possible.

① Start with your immediate family members, friends, and then community.

② Say their names aloud and consider a simple loving act that you could do for them, such as keeping them in your prayers or sending them all ceaseless joy and good health.

③ Take notice of how it feels to open your heart to abundant love for everyone. Do you feel joyful, excited, or hopeful? Do you feel a sense of lightness in your body?

Radical acts of love fan the flames of kindness throughout the world. ♡

may peace find you

The busyness, hurry, and worry of life can easily derail you.

Any sense of a deeper connection with others is often the first thing to go off the tracks.

Learn to use your compassionate qualities to reconnect.

① When you feel distressed, frustrated, or restless, kindly acknowledge that and breathe mindfully for about a minute.

② Set your intention. For example: "May this practice bring me wisdom and ease."

③ Breathe mindfully for a few more breaths.

④ Think of someone who is in pain, is suffering, or is ill. Envision this person as completely as you can.

⑤ Look more deeply. Include any of your own feelings in awareness and hold them with compassion.

⑥ Imagine speaking gently, wishing this person relief. Try saying something like: "May peace find you," or "May you be at ease."

⑦ Let any feelings of mercy guide you. ♡

dump the grudge

I can never forgive him for what happened at Thanksgiving three years ago." You know with absolute certainty that you're holding a grudge when you can recall the exact date, time, and location of a hurtful episode that unleashed your resentment. You also know that grudges are toxic, negative energy that can grow over time and fuel disharmony. Here's a mindful opportunity to liberate your grudges in order to allow the love to flow more freely from within.

① Make a brief mental or written list of the people toward whom you carry resentment.

② These longstanding bitter feelings may be closely attached to a painful memory. Pay attention to the feelings and sensations that arise for you when you revisit that painful memory, person, or situation. Do you feel sadness, shame, or anger? Do you notice any tension mounting in your body, such as in your neck, shoulders, or stomach?

③ Reconnect with the rhythm of your breathing and observe.

④ Say aloud: "I am ready to let go of my grudges in this moment in time. I am ready to reopen myself to more love and more compassion for the things that I cannot change today." Feel free to repeat these words, or your own words, several times over, until they come naturally and comfortably.

This exercise works best when practiced for five minutes each day. The effects will surprise you. ♡

may I be free from pain

Compassion is the opening of your heart to the pain of another.

Have you considered that you could meet any pain in yourself with compassion (instead of anger, fear, or shame)?

Use this practice to explore the territory of self-compassion:

① Give yourself some quiet time and space and breathe mindfully for about a minute.

② Set your intention. For example: "May this practice help me to heal."

③ Breathe mindfully for a few more breaths.

④ Recall and open to some pain you are carrying. It could be physical, emotional, psychological, or from a relationship—anything.

⑤ Breathe mindfully and stay open to your experience. Allow it to be as it is.

⑥ With kindness and compassion, wish yourself relief and ease. For example: "May I be free from suffering," or "May I be at peace."

⑦ Breathe mindfully, gently repeating your phrase as long as you like. ♡

wise love

joy is us together

When you are with your partner, or with dear family members (including pets), allow yourself to connect to and drink deeply of the preciousness in that moment.

Try this practice to help you step back from the distraction of inner busyness and relax into the love that surrounds you:

① Whatever your posture, gently and quietly begin to breathe mindfully.

② Set your intention. For example: "May I feel the love around me in this moment."

③ Breathe mindfully for a few more breaths.

④ Notice any sense of worry, hurry, impatience, or ill ease in your inner life. Acknowledge it kindly and let it go.

⑤ If it helps, gently remind yourself where you are. For example: "This moment, here with those who love me."

⑥ Look and feel more deeply. Rest in the love you feel. ♡

26

forgiveness walk

Forgiveness is a premier healer for resentment and animosity. Take these next few minutes to get outdoors for a vigorous walk toward forgiveness.

① Walk off that potential grudge, work out that pent-up anger, and let loose some bitterness. Pay attention to the pockets of tightness in your body when you're angry, such as your face, chest, or back.

② On this walk, visualize images that make you feel good—a litter of puppies, a warm plate of freshly baked cookies, or

a good, long hug. Now focus on where these good feelings reside in your body, such as the curve of your smile, the softening of your shoulders, or the warmth in your heart.

③ Say aloud: "I am walking to forgive, to have mercy, and to let go of my hostility. When I have forgiveness in my heart, I can move more freely without negative feelings and ill will."

looking at you

How often do you look at your loved one without really seeing her?

Such a failure to connect is usually the result of your attention being focused elsewhere.

Try the following practice of "mindful seeing" to renew and strengthen your connection.

① When you are with your loved one, notice if you are really present and paying attention or not.

② If you are not paying attention, calmly acknowledge that without judging yourself.

③ Quietly set your intention to connect.

④ Breathe mindfully for a few breaths if it helps steady your attention.

⑤ Look gently and more closely at your loved one. See her through eyes of kindness and interest. Notice skin, eyes, hair, expression, clothing, and body posture. Keep breathing mindfully, and relax as you notice more and more.

⑥ How do you feel? Be kind to yourself, too.

⑦ What will happen next? ♡

28

acknowledge every gift

You are surrounded by little, often overlooked gifts every day. How frequently do you remember to acknowledge the giver behind the gift?

① Wherever you are right now, take this moment to focus on a particular time when your partner offered to be helpful or nice to you. He may have tucked in the kids and read them a storybook when you were simply too tired.

② Say aloud: "I am grateful for my partner's kindness and gifts. I give thanks in spirit to him for reminding me of this sacred exchange of kindheartedness."

③ Hold this person in your mind's eye and wish him good tidings, such as prosperity, good health, and happiness.

This is the simple act of gratitude—to acknowledge the giver and to be thankful. ♡

29

may you be well

The words "I love you" can mean many things. The person speaking may even mean something different from what another hears.

Try the following practice—based upon an ancient meditation form called *lovingkindness*—to explore the variety available in "I love you."

① Breathe or listen mindfully for about a minute.

② Set your intention. For example: "May this practice enrich the love I feel and share."

③ Imagine speaking kindly to your loved one, sincerely wishing her well. You might say something like: "May you be happy." "May you be healthy and at ease." "May you be filled with peace." "May you be safe and protected." Use any words you choose.

④ Repeat your phrase slowly, quietly, and lovingly, several times.

⑤ Notice any reactions you feel inside. Honor and respect them.

⑥ What have you learned about "I love you?" What will you say next to your love? ♡

look inside

The Japanese practice of self-reflection, *naikan*, translates to "inside-looking." To practice, you ask yourself three questions every day. Naikan offers a profound way of fostering gratitude by focusing on being present in your life rather than feeling trapped in your daily drama and complaints.

① Ask yourself: "What have I received today?" Hold sacred space in your mind to remember these blessings throughout your day.

② Ask yourself: "What have I given today?" This is your opportunity to acknowledge how you've been generous or helpful to others.

③ Ask yourself: "What trouble have I caused?" Take this moment to recognize your part in the bigger picture of hidden agendas and daily problems.

While Naikan may not solve all your problems, it can help to keep things in perspective. When you reflect on your present situation, you step out of the downward spiral of everyday grievances. This practice has the potential to inspire you to be more giving and more grateful. ♡

holding hands

Love can appear in a simple touch. The physical forms—a hand holding another hand, for example—can reflect deep feelings of love and caring.

Try the following gentle practice of mindful hand-holding to explore the territory of love with your partner:

① When you have a few moments together, take your partner's hand. Tell him what you are doing. Invite him to practice mindfully holding hands with you.

② Breathe mindfully for about a minute. After a few breaths, open and include mindfulness of body sensations.

③ Set your intention. For example: "May this practice deepen our love."

④ Let your attention rest completely on his hand. Hold, squeeze, and caress it, exploring his hand fully, slowly, and gently.

⑤ Notice your own changing sensations with affection.

⑥ Notice any movements in his hand.

⑦ Let love and affection flow from your hands to him. ♡

give thanks for the hard times

Whether or not you believe in God or a higher spirit, when was the last time you prayed to give thanks for all the difficult times in your life? You may give thanks for your new car, for finding the love of your life, or for avoiding a harmful accident. Well, why not for your difficulties, as well? Try this counterintuitive prayer that has amazing effects:

① Either standing or sitting, close your eyes and recall three things that you are truly grateful for. This should be easy.

② Now, add three more things that are painful to recall, such as a difficult divorce, the death of a loved one, or the loss of a friendship.

③ In your prayer, say: "I am thankful for the good and the bad, the love and the hurt. Though I may not know the reason today, even the painful situations will open me to new experiences and the unknown mystery of life."

You may discover surprisingly positive results by making this a daily practice. ♡

laugh out loud

Laughing can quickly bring feelings of joy and connection. It can be good exercise, too!

A great secret to know is that you can just start laughing. You don't even have to think of something funny first.

Try the following practice of laughing out loud with your loved one—for fun!

① Invite your loved one to join you in "laughing practice."

② Begin by mindfully breathing and feeling bodily sensations for about a minute.

③ Set your intention. For example: "May we find happiness and joy together."

④ Let some sounds of laughter start inside and rumble out. Open your gates for some real belly laughs!

⑤ Try "hee-hee-hee" and "ho-ho-ho."

⑥ Laugh back and forth with your partner.

⑦ Laugh together, on purpose, whenever you like. ♡

take a bow

In some cultures, bowing before another person is a greeting and a sign of respect. You can try this next practice on your own or with your partner.

① From a standing position, take your first bow for yourself. This is your opportunity to recognize yourself as part of the vast and mysterious universe.

② Say aloud: "I have the deepest respect for myself."

③ Take a second bow and acknowledge your loved ones, family, friends, and community. Focus on sending them respect and appreciation.

④ Say aloud: "I have the deepest respect for all of my loved ones."

⑤ The last bow is for the miracle of all living things in the universe.

⑥ Say aloud: "I have the deepest respect for the life force that surrounds us all."

Three bows are all it takes for a peaceful moment of respect and gratitude. ♡

affectionate listening

How often is your attention elsewhere when your partner is speaking?

A deeper connection and more joy are close at hand when you replace inattention with affectionate listening.

①   When your partner is speaking to you, notice where your
     attention is. Notice also any feelings of impatience or mental
     "stories" that may be going through your head. Acknowledge
     them and let them go.

② Take a moment to breathe mindfully for a few breaths.

③ Set your intention. For example: "May I be more present for him."

④ As he speaks to you, focus mindfully on the sounds. Notice tone, pace, and volume, as well as meaning.

⑤ Look more closely at him. If you are on a phone, close your eyes and picture him.

⑥ As you listen, let gentle feelings of warmth and affection flow within you.

⑦ Let attention and affection guide your own words in response.

a mile in your partner's shoes

Oftentimes, you may forget what it feels like to walk in your partner's shoes. The next time you are frustrated or disappointed with your partner, try this visualization:

Imagine yourself removing your shoes and putting on your partner's shoes. What are the first things you might notice about them? Are they oversized, faded, or in need of repair?

Consider the miles of life experiences that your partner has walked. Try to imagine the myriad of feelings that she has

experienced in these shoes—agony and despair, confusion and uncertainty, enthusiasm and ecstasy.

Now it's time to slip back into your own shoes and be open to your enormous capacity for empathy and understanding. ♡

love without return

Though expectations are a normal part of everyday life, they have a way of hindering your ability to love more generously. If you don't keep your expectations in check, you will fall victim to negative thinking, such as, "If he really loved me, he would help me more often," or "After all I've done for her out of love, she should at least remember what's important to me." The following practice will aid you in leaving your expectations behind and freeing yourself to give love without expecting something in return:

① In this moment, make a conscious effort to acknowledge a few of your expectations that you put on your partner, family, or friends.

② Consider which expectations are fair and which ones are potentially unrealistic.

③ Now think back on a time in your life when someone was loving to you and you did not feel any obligation attached to it. Often, a best friend can bestow love without attaching responsibility to it.

④ Now, say aloud your affirmation: "I am a loving person. When I give love, there are no hidden strings attached or secret agendas. To love is to give without expecting something in return." ♡

share some silence

What if "being together" actually focused on "being" and not "doing?"

Perhaps a dimension of connectedness—always present, but often unnoticed—might open.

"Being" together could then illumine and enrich all that you "do" together afterward.

Try the following practice—sharing silence mindfully—to explore the territory of connectedness with your partner:

① Ask your partner to join you for these few minutes, and sit or lie down close to each other.

② Breathe mindfully for about a minute.

③ Set your intention. For example: "May this practice together bring us great happiness."

④ Relax and breathe mindfully together. Share the space, silence, and presence together. Let thoughts and busyness go. Just be with each other.

⑤ If you like, when you are ready, smile and touch each other lovingly. ♡

honor your commitments

Wise love recognizes the sanctity of keeping your commitments. Perhaps that is why so many marriage ceremonies include the recitation of vows in the presence of witnesses. But what if you make a pledge to honor your vows daily, rather than just on that one special ceremonial day? Encourage your partner or loved one to participate in this next practice:

① Take a moment to reflect on your top three commitments, such as loyalty, respect, and honesty. Or maybe love, generosity, and friendship.

② Speak your vows aloud to yourself or to your partner. Consider why you selected these three vows and the sense of obligation and importance that they hold in your life and in your relationships.

③ Say aloud to yourself or to your partner: "I pledge to honor my vows to you every day."

This pledge is sacred and contains the everlasting glue that binds a lasting relationship with love. ♡

how can I help?

Being generous of heart toward loved ones or your partner does not have to cost any money.

Generosity manifests through kind attention infused with patience, care, and love.

Generosity is felt especially strongly when attention is consistent, immediate, and without self-interest.

Try offering your attention and help to your partner as an "everyday miracle" in the most common and ordinary interactions.

126

① When your partner calls or asks for your help, ask her to hold on for a moment and go ahead and breathe mindfully for a few breaths.

② Set your intention. For example: "May I give her my attention freely and lovingly."

③ Notice any feelings of impatience or irritation you may be having. Kindly acknowledge them and let them go. Breathe mindfully a bit longer.

④ Turn full attention to her.

⑤ Recognize the blessings of having someone who loves you.

⑥ Respond with kindness: "How can I help?" ♡

41

---

take the good with the bad

Nobody is perfect, right? Whether your relationship is newly forming or you've been together for decades, eventually you'll start tracking all your partner's weaknesses and shortcomings. You may have thought to yourself, "If only she would do it my way, it would be more efficient," or "If he was better at this task, life would be simpler." This train of disapproving thinking can lead to continued disappointment. Try this mindful practice for alleviating blame:

① Make a mental or written list of three things that your partner is not very skilled at, such as cooking, shopping for the kids, or paying the bills on time.

② Make a mental or written list of three things that your partner is really skilled at, such as making house repairs, following instructions, or organizing vacation trips.

③ Do the same for your own personal strengths and weaknesses within the relationship. Be mindful of the kind of compassion and understanding that you would extend to someone else with your limitations.

④ Finally, consider how each of you balances the other.

Love is a two-person job, and you both have what it takes to make it work by loving the whole person, shortcomings and all. ♡

your blessings on me

Openly acknowledging and appreciating everyday gifts from your partner can enrich your relationship.

Turn mindful attention to the routine situations of life with him. Practice feeling and expressing the joy, security, and gratitude you feel.

① Stop, relax, and breathe mindfully for about a minute.

② Set your intention. For example: "May this practice deepen my love for him."

③ Breathe mindfully for a few more breaths.

④ Reflect on your partner. How does he support your life together? Look at "little things" like daily sacrifices, unique gifts and qualities, and contributions to your happiness and well-being.

⑤ Breathe mindfully as you reflect more deeply. Visualize him in action during the day. Feel the ease and happiness his actions evoke in you.

⑥ Thank him, and when you see him again, tell him how good his blessings make you feel. ♡

patience on the journey

If you're accustomed to instant gratification, everything you need at the flick of a switch, your capacity for patience may atrophy like an unused muscle. A sign that impatience has descended is when you start complaining and a feeling of insistence takes over your every thought. You may be thinking to yourself, "I wish she'd hurry up," or, "He takes forever to finish his chores." The next five-minute meditation will instill a little endurance for just those times:

① Take this moment to stop everything you're doing. Find a place to sit and shut out the world, if possible.

② As you begin to quiet your mind, try to visualize exactly where your patience resides in your body. Perhaps it's on vacation in your mind or has left your body altogether.

③ Consider a time when you were not in a hurry, not anxious for your partner to get up to speed. A time when you were simply at ease and serene with the natural flow of life.

④ Say your intentions aloud: "I am calling forth the calm winds of patience. May patience always be a lasting and enduring presence in my life."

When you usher in your patience, love and understanding are sure to break through. ♡

holding you

Life happens only in the present moment.

The present moment is the only time you can be with the one you love.

Let mindfulness help you connect more deeply the next time you hold her close.

1. While embracing your loved one, relax and take a few mindful breaths.

2. Acknowledge the preciousness of this moment, and set your intention to be fully present.

3. Continue the embrace, breathing mindfully and allowing yourself to relax and open to your experience.

4. Gently bring mindful attention to each changing sensation, sound, scent, and taste as it happens. Let each experience come to you and fill you. Let each one go.

5. When your attention moves into past or future thinking, gently bring it back to the experiences happening here and now. Relax.

6. Drink deeply of the sweetness in this moment. ♡

stars of compassion

The Dalai Lama believes that if you meditate on compassion for others, the first beneficiary will be you. And the Buddha believed that when you love yourself, you cannot bring harm to another. Compassion starts with you. It is a steady reminder that others are also suffering, and so you are not alone. This meditation will guide you along your path toward greater empathy and happiness.

① What does compassion mean to you? Reflect on what it means to have empathy, understanding, and concern for others. For some, it is an empathetic awareness of the complexity of difficult situations and the complicated feelings that arise.

② Consider a time when you were compassionate. Did you comfort someone after a painful breakup? Did you make a donation to a natural-disaster relief organization?

③ What emotions are you experiencing right now? Openheartedness? Sympathy? Love?

④ Now consider a time when someone showed compassion toward you. Perhaps a friend gave extra emotional support during a tender time in your life.

These are the stars of compassion that light our path along our journey toward happiness. ♡

46

extraordinary love songs

So easily the energy and mood in relationships can become stuck in the serious and practical.

But lightness and humor are closer than you might think.

Shift toward fun by adding a soundtrack at some unexpected moment!

① When you and your partner are busy doing some chore together, quietly take a mindful breath.

② Set your intention. For example: "May this practice make us laugh."

③ Softly start singing out loud about what you are doing. Add drama and volume. Be romantic. Be funny. Sing with gusto.

④ Add some phrases like "and I love you," or, "I can't live without you," or, "and you are beautiful."

⑤ When you cannot be with your partner, imagine singing to her. Laugh and enjoy. ♡

47

be an ally

Love alone doesn't make you a terrific friend. In fact, you may forget all about the virtues of friendship after a significant amount of time drifts by in any relationship. Don't let yourself get steered away from the necessity of maintaining a meaningful friendship with the one you love. Here's how to become a loving ally:

① Though you may love your partner more than anyone on the planet, be mindful of times when you are not treating him with the respect that you would instinctively show your friends.

② Take a few moments to consider three virtues of friendship that are important to you, such as being kind, nonjudgmental, or supportive. Reflect on the meaning of these three revered qualities.

③ Say aloud: "I value friendship as a vital component in every relationship." Now insert your three virtues into this sentence and let the words encircle your mind: "I strive to be _____, _____, and _____ with my partner and loved ones every day." ♡

48

appreciate the differences

Having patience with each other protects your relationship.

Take some time to relax, reflect, and appreciate how his ways are different from yours, and celebrate these differences.

The rewards can be sweet.

① Give yourself some time. Choose a comfortable place and breathe mindfully for about a minute.

② Set your intention. For example: "May this practice grow our love."

③ Allow yourself to continue softening and opening as you breathe mindfully for a few more breaths.

④ Bring his image into your heart and mind.

⑤ Remember how he does some things differently from you. Think of an example. Acknowledge any irritation you feel. Breathe mindfully as you reflect.

⑥ Look more closely. See how his way reflects inner qualities that are deep, unique, and especially true for him.

⑦ Looking deeply, can you now appreciate more beauty and richness in the differences? ♡

a spoonful of reassurance

Reassurance is the swiftest remedy for a troubled soul. When you offer comfort and assurance to someone facing an agonizing situation, you are imparting one of the greatest gifts of loving kindness and friendship.

Let's practice it right now! Here are a few suggestions for how to be supportive of and comforting to someone you love:

- Write your partner a note reminding her that you care, that everything will work out, and that you will remain by her side through hard times.

- Offer comfort through a hug, a phone call, a flower offering.

- Show your support by sending an e-mail or text message to find out how she's doing when she's going through a rough time.

- Acknowledge your partner's accomplishments, both big and small.

Remember to extend these comforting and supportive gestures to yourself when you're having a stressful day. ♡

here for you

Your presence is a priceless gift. Yet staying present, especially when your dear one is in pain or is upset, oftentimes can be extremely challenging.

This practice could help you stay present for his pain and offer him more support.

① When your partner is in pain or brings some difficulty to you, breathe mindfully for a few breaths.

② Set your intention. For example: "May I remain present and supportive for him."

③ As he speaks about what's bothering him, listen mindfully and allow yourself to relax.

④ Notice any impulse to interrupt, give premature advice, or criticize, and let it go. Keep breathing. Relax. Stay present. Listen mindfully.

⑤ Acknowledge all you hear with attentive, loving silence or with simple phrases like, "I wish things could be better," or, "I'm sorry things are so bad."

⑥ Let mindfulness and compassion guide your words and actions. ♡

appreciate the little things

Everyone's guilty of it. You're trudging along through your numbing routine and forget to show your partner how much you truly appreciate her. Get out of the rut of taking each other for granted by doing this one together. The following exercise will help guide you on your road toward gratitude:

① Take notice of the little things first. Being mindful of the flowers blooming outside or the trickle of winter sunlight through your window or the sound of your children giggling

in their bedroom will put you at the starting gate for opening your heart to appreciate all that surrounds you.

② Now make a mental list of things your partner does that you really appreciate, things such as making coffee every morning, running an errand for you, or paying for dinner.

③ Let your feelings of gratitude swell up in your body, perhaps starting with a smile. Let the gratitude heat up in your heart and wiggle down into your toes.

④ Say aloud to yourself or your partner, "I am thankful for all the little things you do to make my life easier and sweeter."

love in action

no pain, no blame

Have you ever noticed how often the desire to blame someone arises from your own feelings of pain and upset?

While responsibility and accountability are vital in healthy relationships, unfair criticism and blame are toxic.

Try the following practice the next time you feel hurt and want to blame someone:

① Breathe or listen mindfully for about a minute.

② Include your body sensations in your mindful attention. Notice especially your throat, chest, and abdomen.

③ Let your attention be filled with kindness and compassion.

④ Set your intention. For example: "May my pain not drive me to harm another."

⑤ Breathe, listen, or notice sensations mindfully for a few more breaths.

⑥ Notice any angry or blaming thoughts or stories you may be having. Let them go. Stop feeding or following them. Don't blame yourself for any thoughts you may have, either.

⑦ Decide on the wisest action only after attending to your own pain. ♡

take a "shake-it" break

Searing blowups with a loved one can cause a chain reaction of stress and anxiety. Anger has a way of tipping the scales away from the things that you truly value the most in life, such as kindness, empathy, and compromise. A preprogrammed shake-it break can help both of you dissipate the rage. Try it together, if you can.

①　When tension and anger reach a boiling point, instead of dragging it out indefinitely, negotiate about taking a break, scheduling a time to discuss it later, and then each of you go for a walk or get outside. In the heat of the moment, both of

you give yourself permission to walk away without needing to solve everything immediately. How many arguments ever got resolved during a screaming match?

② Once you've walked away with the agreement that you'll work on it later with your partner, find a quiet place to try this physical exercise. Begin by standing up and shaking out every single part of your body. Come on, don't be self-conscious! Be methodical as you wiggle and jiggle your head, neck, shoulders, arms, wrists, fingers, chest, torso, hips, stomach, legs, ankles, and toes.

③ Keep up your movement while you shake out your heavy thoughts and feelings. Imagine all this vibration allowing your anger and hurt to trickle out through your ears.

Don't let anger and resentment destabilize your relationship. Make wiggle room for putting your best foot forward in the direction of resolution. ♡

54

offer forgiveness

As human beings in relationships, we inevitably hurt each other, intentionally or unintentionally. That is why *forgiveness* is so important. When another hurts you, you have the choice of holding resentment or offering forgiveness.

Forgiveness is "offered" because you have no control over whether or not the other will accept it.

Offering forgiveness is *not* an invitation for the other to hurt you again, but is instead a means of releasing your own hurt.

You can explore offering forgiveness with this practice.

① Breathe or listen mindfully for about a minute.

② Set your intention. For example: "May I learn more about forgiveness."

③ Recall some hurt you felt from another.

④ Imagine speaking to him, saying: "I offer you forgiveness."

⑤ Repeat this phrase several times and kindly notice your own inner responses.

⑥ What do you learn? What needs to happen next? ♡

greeting ritual

If you have a pet, then you know the heightened sense of enthusiasm, loyalty, and utter devotion that your pet displays upon your arrival. Take notes! You can make a better effort of greeting your loved one when he comes home. Be aware of the urge to insist on immediately talking about pressing matters, such as a bill to pay or something that needs to be fixed. Try out one of the following greeting rituals to infuse the moment with love:

- "I am so glad you're home! You fill my life with joy."

- "It's been a long day. Let's support each other through the last part of it."

- "I've missed you all day. I'm so thankful that you made it home safely."

- "It's always so good to see you. You still make me melt with love."

- "There's so much to talk about; but first, let's just be loving and supportive to each other."

- "Our troubles can wait. I just want to give you a long hug and tell you how much I cherish you." ♡

ask forgiveness

Resentment can damage a relationship—often severely.

As human beings, we are bound to cause hurt in relationships, whether we mean to or not.

A potent expression of love in action is to acknowledge your own hurtful actions or words and to apologize and ask for forgiveness.

The following practice is a way for you to explore the act of asking for forgiveness:

1. Give yourself some private space and time. Breathe or listen mindfully for about a minute.

2. Set your intention. For example: "May this practice help me strengthen my relationships."

3. Think of someone you have hurt, whether intentionally or unintentionally.

4. Imagine speaking to that person. For example: "For any harm I may have caused you, I ask your forgiveness."

5. With compassion, repeat the phrase a few times and notice your responses.

6. What do you discover? What will you do now? ♡

anchor of love

If someone you love suffers from depression or another mental health challenge, then you know firsthand the pressures it can bring to a relationship. Her erratic mood swings can affect you on a day-to-day basis. Let love in to guide your heart toward compassion and hope with this next practice:

① Positive and negative emotions will fluctuate with the seasons, often without any provocation. Avoid the tendency to try to predict someone's emotional outbursts. Don't blame yourself or mind-read.

② Think back on a couple of occasions when she was content, calm, and generally happy. Perhaps it was the last weekend getaway or at the birth of your child.

③ The next time your loved one is feeling out of sorts, let her just be. Let her emotions take their natural course.

④ Say aloud or to yourself: "This is a very difficult time for you. I'm here to be an anchor and support you. It will pass."

⑤ Love her through this painful eruption. Remind yourself that you cannot fix someone else but you *can* lovingly support her through a difficult time. ♡

58

turn off the autopilot

The constant daily routine can turn many couples into something like robots, operating on a sort of autopilot. It's time to mindfully reconnect and take a break from your habit. Take this moment to stop yourself midstream in your routine and do something different. Here are some suggestions:

- If you watch TV after work every night, go for a walk with your partner instead.

- If you always start a bunch of chores before you make dinner, take a break from your multitasking and invite your partner to sit and have a cup of tea with you.

- Ask your partner to share something good about his day.

- Remind your partner of five things that you really appreciate about him.

- Invite your partner to be playful and pretend your couch is a hot tub, or a waterbed, or that you've just dived into a refreshing lake and come up for air.

- Ask your partner to be spontaneous with you and break out of a lifeless routine right now! ♡

forgive yourself

In the hurt and pain of relationships, it is easy to overlook the need to include yourself when offering and asking for forgiveness.

Try the following practice to explicitly include yourself in the healing power of forgiveness:

① Breathe or listen mindfully for about a minute.

② Set your intention. For example: "May this practice promote healing in me."

③ Breathe or listen mindfully for a few more breaths.

④ Recall a situation where you either caused or felt hurt in a relationship.

⑤ Without getting lost in the story, and as compassionately as you can, speak gently to yourself. Say something like: "For any hurt I may have caused, intentional or unintentional, I offer myself forgiveness."

⑥ Repeat your phrase a few times, noticing your inner responses.

⑦ Acknowledge and learn from *all* of the responses. ♡

60

---

work together

For the most part, it makes sense to do house chores separately. It's time efficient for your partner to repair something outside while you're doing the laundry. But a relationship isn't always about productivity and efficiency. It's about finding imaginative ways to foster romance within your connection on a day-to-day basis. Take five minutes to share your chores:

- Wash and dry the dishes together.

- Fold the laundry together.

- Prepare a meal together.

- Scrub the kitchen floor together.

- Do yard work together.

- Make the bed together.

- Reorganize a cluttered drawer together.

- Clean all the windows of the car together.

- Clear the dinner table and put all the food away together.

- Dust a room together.

- Make a to-do list together.

- Clean the bathroom together.

- Play hooky on your chores together. ♡

safe with me

One of the greatest gifts you can offer another is a feeling of safety in your company.

By learning to better manage your own disturbing states of anger and fear, you make your presence safer and more inviting to others.

Try this practice for working with your own anger and fear:

1. When you notice you are upset or angry, mindfully offer compassion to yourself.

2. Breathe, listen, or move mindfully for about a minute.

3. Set your intention. For example: "May I manage my own anger and upset wisely."

4. Stop fighting the anger or fear. Stop feeding it, too. Try making space for it. Feel it in your body. Whatever you feel, breathe mindfully with it.

5. Notice any anger- or fear-driven thoughts. Don't fight or feed them, either. Acknowledge them and let them go. Breathe mindfully with them.

6. End by offering yourself an affirmation. For example: "I am stronger and wiser than this upset."

7. Move forward. ♡

waves of serenity

Mounting stress can charge into your life like it owns the place, taking over your mind and body. It can disrupt your relationship and trigger a whole set of unrelated disputes over the most inconsequential stuff. When that next stressor occurs, try out this relaxing visualization.

Stop the madness and find a quiet place to sit and close your eyes. On your next slow breath out, feel the waves of air moving away from you, leaving your lungs emptied. Check in with your shoulders and make sure they aren't attached to your ears.

As you breathe in, focus on breathing from your belly, as if it were a balloon expanding and contracting with each breath. Now imagine that on each inhale you are floating away from your worries and tension. You are drifting off across the skyline, distancing yourself from your troubles. As you exhale, imagine waves of serenity surging through you.

Move gently throughout your day. ♡

free from it all

Many couples are in the position of caring for their elderly family members. Caretakers experience excessive stress, which can drain your energy reserves for other loved ones who need you, too. The following exercise will help to relieve your stored-up mental strain and refuel you for the journey to be more loving:

① Begin with simple stretching movements for igniting the blood flow and releasing tension. Place both arms over your head and reach for the sky, and then gently drop your arms

and bend your body to hang over your toes. Try this a few times.

② Now take a minute to check in with yourself. Are you exhausted and depleted? Overwhelmed and feeling under attack? Anxious and spread too thin?

③ Give yourself permission to let it all go. For five whole minutes, if you can, you are not responsible for anything or anyone.

④ Say aloud your affirmation: "In this moment, I am not in control of every detail. I am taking care of just myself right now, so that I can return with more affection and better attention for others." ♡

what is really going on?

When your partner becomes angry, do you ever feel frustrated as you talk and listen to her?

Effectively managing your own reactions in the midst of such difficult moments is the first step toward better support and help for her.

The following practice could be a new approach for both of you:

① When you are faced with an angry partner, resolve to try something different.

② Breathe mindfully for about a minute.

③ Set your intention. For example: "May this practice support me and help her."

④ Collect and steady yourself by breathing mindfully and letting your body relax a bit.

⑤ Acknowledge her anger quietly to yourself, then change the word "anger" to "pain." Begin to see, hear, and feel her anger as pain instead.

⑥ Mindfully notice what is happening inside of you as you recognize the pain.

⑦ Respond wisely to the pain. ♡

warming the cold silences

Every couple knows the old silent-treatment game. You're both at a standoff in a dispute, and your last move is to go silent. At this point, you may even notice a slight frosty chill in the room. Warm up your heart and your relationship with the following exercise:

① On the next occasion that you feel yourself shutting down, take your silent retreat as an opportunity to seek understanding and compromise instead of building a better argument for round two.

② Consider both sides of the disagreement or situation and acknowledge that there may be many different angles of interpretation, depending on how you look at it.

③ Make a mental or written list of a few ways that you would be willing to be flexible in trying to resolve the issues involved.

④ When calm has been restored, let your partner or loved one know that ultimately you seek compromise and resolution.

The art of reconciliation takes practice and commitment on both sides. ♡

fishing for feelings

Do you have difficulty expressing what is on your mind or difficulty communicating your feelings? We all do, occasionally. During times of conflict or unresolved issues, you may experience undue emotional stress and be overwhelmed, making it troublesome to articulate what you truly feel. Let this next visualization help you unwind from the enormity of your situation in order to find your way back to what's in your heart.

Imagine you are setting off in a small rowboat into a very peaceful and still lake. No motorboats, no water skiers—only you and your fishing pole. Even if you don't know how to fish, you instinctively recall that you gently fling your baited line into the water and then reel in the line after a moment. Picture yourself fishing. Each time you throw out your line, visualize tossing out your troubles and unwinding your worries. Each time you wind up the fishing line, imagine spooling in your feelings. When you quiet the mind, you make space for feelings to emerge. What kinds of emotions are surfacing from your crystal clear waters?

anger and fear

Being emotionally intelligent includes developing skills of sensitive and accurate self-awareness.

Every loving relationship encounters frustration, disagreements, and anger.

By learning to look more deeply, you can often find some fear beneath any anger you feel. It may be the fear that is actually driving you.

Try the following practice to explore the territory of anger and fear more fully:

① When you are feeling angry about something in your relationship, when you can, gracefully step back and give yourself some space.

② Breathe or move mindfully for about a minute.

③ Set your intention. For example: "May this practice bring me wisdom and peace."

④ Kindly and mindfully revisit the upsetting situation in your imagination. Breathe mindfully as you do this.

⑤ When you feel anger return, ask kindly: "What is my deeper fear in this situation?"

⑥ Listen with compassion for all of your responses. ♡

to each his own style

If you have children, then you've likely experienced disagreement over parenting styles. One of you may prefer a hard-line, firm approach, while the other may favor a more hands-off, subtler method. Each style has its pros and cons. This exercise works best if both of you are involved, if possible.

① Seated at a table across from each other, close your eyes and reconnect with the rhythm of your breathing.

② Now open your eyes and speak your intentions aloud, such as: "With this practice, I am opening myself to make room for creative resolution for this situation."

③ Make a mental or written list of three positive things about your partner's approach and then ask your partner to do the same for you.

④ How does it feel to hear your approach praised for its merit by your partner? Do you feel heard and understood?

Conflict resolution requires being a good listener and communicator. When you and your partner commit to acknowledging strengths, you shift the focus away from your parenting styles and back onto what's best for your children. ♡

fighting for control

How often do disagreements with your partner come down to a need to be in control?

And how often is the need to be in control rooted in a need to be right, or responsible, or perfect?

As soon as such neediness arises, a golden opportunity for freedom from it also arises.

Try the following practice when you are caught in a battle for control:

① Breathe mindfully for a few breaths and compassionately acknowledge that a part of you is struggling for control.

② Set your intention. For example: "May I understand and relax the part of me that needs control."

③ Tune in mindfully to your body. Feel the location and sensations of the struggle. Breathe into each place gently and kindly. Relax as much as you can safely.

④ Ask quietly: "What am I trying to control? Why? What if I didn't try to control that?"

⑤ Listen patiently for all of your responses. Act on them wisely.

♡

end the tug-of-war

Jealousy can be a dangerous and emotional beast, when let loose. You may experience tunnel vision and blind rage. The slightest provocation can unleash a fury that should not be wrestled with. Whether your suspicions are confirmed or unsubstantiated, the first order for repair is to rebuild trust with your partner. Follow these mindful steps for opening communication and restoring trust:

① You may be experiencing a tug-of-war with fear and anxiety. Take this moment to imagine dropping the rope, and allow yourself to become an observer.

② In your observing stance, practice living in the present moment. The future and outcome are many miles away. There is only you, and this room, and these walls, and your thoughts.

③ Be aware of when your mind is assisting you in finding clarity and when it is not. Your stress and worries need not be an obstacle to seeking the answers you need and the reassurance that you desire.

④ When you begin to feel a calmness settle over you, you are ready to ask for reassurance and to build trust with the one you love. ♡

mindful listener

Amidst your hurried and on-the-go lifestyle, do you really make time to listen actively, taking in what the other person is saying and then repeating it back to him without judgment? A mindful listener requires practice in order to master the skills to really be present in the dialogue. Here are communication strategies for strengthening the conscious listener in you:

① Begin by being silent and letting the other person speak. Allow him to complete his thoughts and sentences before you interrupt or interject.

② Avoid getting distracted by other issues. Continue to focus your attention on the current concerns of the other person.

③ Next, ask for clarification. You may say: "This is what I heard you say. Is that what you meant?"

④ When your partner has had sufficient time to share, take your turn being heard.

Listening conscientiously provides a good role model for how you wish to be heard and understood. ♡

impatience is not you

Patience for your partner is an active ingredient in the deep and trusting love you share.

What if you could cultivate more patience?

You could begin with mindful attention and compassion for your own impatience.

① When you notice yourself feeling impatient or irritated with your partner, take a time-out and breathe mindfully for about a minute.

② Set your intention. For example: "May this practice strengthen our trust in each other."

③ Breathe mindfully for a few more breaths. Concentrate your focus closely on each breath sensation.

④ Shift attention to the physical sensations associated with feeling impatient. Feel the sensations in your body. Breathe and allow them.

⑤ Notice any thoughts or judgments in your mind. You don't have to fight or feed them. Just notice and allow.

⑥ See how the sensations and thoughts of impatience arise and fade. Impatience is not you. ♡

time spent apart

If you and your loved one spend a great deal of time apart, due perhaps to different work schedules or frequent business trips, then you know how challenging it can be to try to infuse every conversation with positive energy and loving kindness. In fact, couples frequently forget to say, "I love you." Make time to reconnect in creative, loving ways, even if it's via the phone or e-mail. Here's how:

① Keep in mind that every interaction with a loved one has the potential to be sacred.

② Take this conscious moment to consider what your interaction would be like if you knew it was your last. Consider five or six loving things you could remind your loved one of.

③ Speak or write three of those heartfelt expressions right now. This cannot wait until tomorrow!

④ If you have trouble formulating the right words, you might try, "I love you more than life itself." "I love you with all my heart and soul." "I am so grateful to have you in my life." Or, "You mean the world to me, and I miss you every day that you're away." ♡

bedtime blessing

With dual-career households and the demands of parenting, couples often complain of not having enough quality time for each other. When you finally do gather to unwind at the end of the day, it doesn't help that you may be competing with the TV, school homework, and a half-dozen phone calls to return. Don't let your evening tasks rob you of a few precious minutes to meditate together. It might just become a part of your nightly routine:

① Before you collapse into bed tonight, kneel at your bedside or sit up in your bed and take a few moments to count your blessings.

② Take a minute or two to contemplate silently three good things that happened to you today or things you were grateful for. Now share aloud your gratitude and blessing to your partner. Continue to express your gratitude aloud to your partner by saying: "It is a gift to share this life with you. I am thankful for this moment to be here with you and to lie next to you." This back-and-forth exchange between you and your partner is an opportunity to fan the flames of appreciation.

③ Let the return of silence to your bedroom be a quiet reminder of how precious your time is together. ♡

cherishing life

75

invitation for love

Throughout Asian culture, the century-old tea ceremony is an invitation for love.

① Make one cup of tea and place it between the two of you. Sit across from each other at the table.

② Face each other while each of you gently grasps the cup, overlapping hands and fingers. Make eye contact and take notice of the tendrils of steam rising from the cup, the heat between your fingers, and the tenderness of your partner's fingers interlaced in yours.

③ Say aloud the following prayer or make up your own: "This cup of tea is an invitation for love. It is infused with our belief in the magic of our bond."

④ Offer a sip to your partner and vice versa. Feel the warmth trickle into your whole body.

⑤ Now give each other a brief moment of silence to just be here and enjoy this special connection. ♡

76

dear stranger

Wise ones say we are more alike than different.

It can be amazing and uplifting to open to this possibility through the simple act of mindful attention to others.

See what discoveries you can make with the following practice, alone or with your partner.

① When you are in a public place, breathe or listen mindfully for about a minute.

② Set your intention. For example: "May this practice awaken curiosity and wonder in me."

③ Bring your attention gently to someone you see. Without doing anything that signals to him or makes him uncomfortable, simply observe him mindfully.

④ Notice and let go of any reactive judgments or stories your mind creates.

⑤ Imagine him as an infant, a child, as he is now, elderly, dying.

⑥ See him as someone, like you, who wishes to be happy.

⑦ If you like, silently wish him well. ♡

bed magic

For most couples, the bedroom is a sacred place. In that very bed, you may have been proposed to, or conceived children, or held each other tightly through sorrows and tears. Make the bed together, if possible, and be mindful of the private beauty of this act.

①   As you pull the sheets taut, consider how every thread contains a memory of all the nights you've lain together.

②   As you fluff up the pillow, imagine the countless dreams that have seeped into it.

③ When you straighten the blanket, think of all the warmth and safety that you've felt beneath it.

④ When you arrange the bedspread, do you recall the reason you chose the particular color or pattern?

⑤ If you have extra throw pillows, pretend that you are anointing your bed as if it were a holy temple.

⑥ Say aloud: "May our love sleep restfully each night and arise with new vitality and vibrancy each morning." ♡

78

elemental truth

The wisdom of many cultures points to the view that all life forms share elemental qualities: earth, water, fire, wind, and space.

Try on this view for yourself and see what you might discover. Consider inviting your partner to join you.

① Find a comfortable spot—indoors or out—where you can easily connect with the natural world. For example, you could be sitting or standing near a flower, stone, or houseplant; or on a beach, near a stream, or in a wood.

② Breathe or listen mindfully for about a minute.

③ Set your intention. For example: "May this practice awaken awe and wonder in me."

④ For the rest of this practice, mindfully tune in to each of your senses as you connect with the solidity of the earth, the dampness of water, the warmth of fire, the movement of wind, and the stillness of space in and around you.

⑤ When the elements come to you, smile at them. Then, let them go. What do they teach? ♡

79

miracles of life

For many of you, family meals may not be the picture-perfect ideal that you wish them to be— you're stuck in the kitchen while the kids crowd around the TV. Create a simple family ritual for instilling your love and values back into this sacred mealtime. Nothing formal—just be creative. Here's an idea to get you started:

①   Seated together and before you eat, light a candle. The person who lights the candle starts by saying what he or she is thankful for in the moment. You may say, "I am thankful to have my family here," or, "I am thankful for this wonderful food on my plate."

②   Pass the candle to each person until everyone has had a chance to give thanks.

If you make this ritual a regular part of your dinner routine, it will become a family tradition, reminding each of you of the miracles of life that we often overlook. ♡

80

flames of romance

Whether you experience the fatigue that sometimes arises in a long-term relationship or just feel too drained of energy at the end of the night for lovemaking, fanning the flames of intimacy is challenging for all couples. Here are a few creative ideas for invigorating your romantic connection:

- Coax your partner to bed a little earlier than usual and slip her a thoughtful love note, reminding her how much you care.

- If you have different sleep schedules, ask her to tuck you in tonight, the way you might with a child—making the child feel safe, protected, and surrounded by your love at all times.

- Before bed, take five minutes to hold each other with your hearts wide open. Be enveloped in your partner's warmth, tenderness, and sheltering arms.

- Despite how tired or cranky you might be feeling, take a few minutes to end your night with a silent prayer, acknowledging the magnificent forces of love that conspired to bring you two together. ♡

no ill will

Without realizing it or meaning to, you can be hijacked by frustration and ill will into a painful place of criticizing life rather than cherishing it.

It's easy to feel judgment, blame, and even anger toward others. You could be in a situation with your loved one, or somewhere else, like waiting in line or being stuck in traffic.

Try the following practice the next time a difficult situation inspires those painful feelings:

① Notice any ill will you feel. Acknowledge it, and breathe or listen mindfully for about a minute.

② Set your intention. For example: "May this practice restore my connections with life."

③ Speak kindly to yourself. Say something like: "May I be happy, healthy, peaceful, and safe." Repeat this several times.

④ Look around you at others. Include them: "May you be happy, healthy, peaceful, and safe."

⑤ Practice caring for your ill will whenever necessary. ♡

82

hand in hand

Don't let another day go by without dancing together. A slow dance can deepen your romance and replenish the heart with more love. Drop what you're doing this instant and make it happen. Keep these few items in mind as you move your bodies in leisurely rhythm:

- If you picked out music, think back on why you chose it. What memories does it hold for you?

- Be aware of how his body feels next to yours. Think about how it feels to have his hand on the small of your back, or intimacy created by linking your hands together. Do you like to be spun around, or do you prefer rocking slowly with your face buried in his neck?

- What emotions stir inside you when you move with him?

- Give him a compliment right now on his twinkling eyes, gorgeous smile, or generous heart. ♡

thankful for you

It is so easy to overlook the everyday blessings of a good relationship. Just being in each other's company can be such a gift.

Try the following practice spontaneously when you are together with your partner but engaged in different activities:

① Stop whatever you are doing and breathe or listen mindfully for about a minute.

② Set your intention. For example: "May this practice deepen my love for (say her name)."

③ Without disturbing her, focus your kind and mindful attention on her.

④ Hear her sounds. See her shape, color, and movements.

⑤ Feel her presence in your life right now, in this moment.

⑥ Breathe or listen mindfully for a few more breaths, aware of her presence. Allow yourself to relax and inhabit this moment as fully as possible.

⑦ Acknowledge and appreciate the gift of her love.

⑧ Try including other dear ones in this practice whenever you like. ♡

84

altar of love

A great many places of worship contain altars, or sacred spaces for ornaments to reside and where ceremonies are performed. Why not create one in your home as a symbol of your magical connection with loved ones?

① Keep it simple and small—perhaps just a tiny box covered in colorful cloth with a single candle above your mantel, with maybe a photo that represents togetherness or that makes your heart smile inside.

② Each night before you sleep, light the candle alone or with someone you love and recognize the inherent beauty of your altar for love. Consider what it means to take this tranquil time to honor your loving relationships.

③ Speak your intentions: "I light this candle to remind me that I am blessed with loving people in my life."

May your altar be a guidepost that always leads back to your openness to love and gratitude. ♡

abundant love

Despite how painful it is to lose a loved one, love is infinite. Love is not a resource that dries up or goes out of business. In fact, there is enough love for everyone on the planet. Take this mindful moment to acknowledge the unlimited love that already exists in your life.

① Begin with your family. Make a mental list of past and present family members who love you, such as your grandparents, mother, father, brother, sister, partner, and children.

②   Move outward in this circle of endless love and list your friends, roommates, and distant relatives. And don't forget your pets.

③   Extending further, include past partners and lovers.

④   Open yourself to the vast list of things that remind you of love's presence, such as old love letters; love stories in books, poems, or movies; or a walk on the beach in the summertime with your partner.

Try this exercise any time you need to be reminded of love's unlimited presence in your life. ♡

your family circle

There can be great power in remembering and acknowledging your extended family and the common bonds running, literally, as blood through your veins.

Which talents, interests, even foibles, are shared with ancestors and relations?

Visiting your "family circle" mindfully can feed a deeper appreciation of your connection to life, too.

① Breathe or listen mindfully for about a minute.

② Set your intention. For example: "May this practice enrich and nurture me."

③ Reflect gently on a specific talent or gift of yours.

④ Recall a relative or ancestor who shared that gift. Imagine he or she is with you.

⑤ Think of other gifts or qualities. Imagine a circle of your family members surrounding you, whenever you need them, sharing gifts, strengths, and challenges.

⑥ Feel their presence and support deep in your veins. ♡

embrace your differences

During times of duress, have you ever noticed how your mind will focus on all the differences between you and the one you love? You'll find yourself easily annoyed by the smallest habits or quirks until nothing he can do is good enough. You may even wish for him to change. Practicing the next exercise can help you abandon the idea that people can be forced into a box of your making.

① Differences are what make you uniquely marvelous. Take this moment to consciously recognize how dissimilarities are the rare elements in any relationship that keep things interesting and compelling.

② Imagine looking through your loved one's eyes and consider: What does this person yearn for? What private revelations has he experienced? What does he daydream about? Does he have any regrets that you know of? What are his deepest doubts and fascinations?

③ This is your opportunity to fully embrace the mystery and awe of your relationship and to steer clear of energy spent wishing for your partner to change into something he'll never be. ♡

88

may you always be happy

The happiness and joy of your partner (and other loved ones) is especially precious and offers you a well of deep joy.

Learn to drink mindfully from that well, sharing their joy in the present moment.

① When your partner is nearby doing something else and you notice her smiling or laughing, turn your attention there and breathe mindfully.

②   Set your intention quietly. For example: "May this practice bring us both great joy."

③   Let your attention move closer and deeper. See her smiling and relaxing. Hear her laughing. Feel her happiness.

④   Breathe mindfully and let yourself become even more relaxed and receptive. Notice a smile or a laugh of your own.

⑤   If you like, wish her happiness always. For example: "May you always be happy," or, "May you be filled with joy and peace."

⑥   Savor your joy. ♡

89

be vulnerable

So much of your daily life forces you to construct elaborate walls so others can't get in or to protect you from being seen for who you truly are. You may appear stoic and unaffected on the outside when you are actually scared and desperate on the inside. While this may be appropriate at work or with strangers, it doesn't have to be this way with loved ones. Learn to be vulnerable in order to allow others to help you.

① First, remind yourself that expressing your feelings and showing vulnerability are not signs of weakness. In fact, it takes great courage to invite others to be there for you, to offer emotional support.

② Take this moment to ask for help. You don't have to be alone in your struggle. Call a friend, trust him with your emotions, and break down the walls that only divide you from others.

③ If this is new territory for you, then be gentle with yourself. Ask for reassurance and comfort. ♡

90

prayers for animals

Humans have a deep and ancient connection with other animals. Examples of prayers for animals can be found in many cultures and in diverse faith traditions.

Human prayers for animals have asked that the animals be relieved from suffering, fear, and hunger. They have requested guidance for human hearts and hands to be filled with compassion and kindness toward other creatures, and that all humans become true friends to animals.

① When you are moved or feel a special connection with an animal, stop and acknowledge that, feeling it deeply.

② Collect your attention and strengthen your presence with a few mindful breaths.

③ Set your intention. For example: "May this practice deepen my connection with all living things."

④ Focus mindful attention on the connection you feel in this moment.

⑤ Listen inwardly for any words or wishes you have for this or other animals.

⑥ Offer your words and wishes consciously, with kindness and respect. ♡

too much work, not enough play

Work without play makes for a dull, predictable life. Invigorate your relationship by making playtime a priority, even if you only have five minutes to spare. Here are a few ideas to ignite spontaneity in your drab routine:

- Try "competitive dating," where each partner tries to outdo the previous date's level of fun. Coax your partner or loved one into playing along.

- Try something you used to do as a kid, such as miniature golf, ice-skating, roller-skating, or check out a 3-D movie.

- Order tickets for something new or that you have never tried before, such as a musical, stand-up comedy, or the performance of a dance troupe.

- Arm wrestle for love—the winner has to give you a hundred kisses starting at your head and working her way down!

- Run, skip, and hold hands down the sidewalk. You might feel silly, but you know you'll start to laugh at yourself. ♡

say yes to life

Y es" is a popular and widespread gesture of joyful agreement and hearty acceptance.

"Y-E-S!"

Saying yes is often accompanied by a vigorous sort of physical gesture—or two.

Saying yes is a potent way of aligning with and joining.

Try saying yes to the ever-changing, mysterious flow of life through the present moment.

① Breathe mindfully for about a minute.

② Set your intention. For example: "May this practice give me happiness and energy."

③ Breathe mindfully for a few more breaths.

④ Notice and gently name the different experiences as they arise in this moment. As you name each one, simply say yes. For example, "Worried thoughts—yes." "Noisy outside—yes." "Ache in the back—yes."

⑤ For each experience, gently whisper yes without fighting, intellectualizing, or resisting. Just say yes.

⑥ What do you notice? ♡

93

stairway of dreams

Every couple goes through times when dreams and needs yank you each in different directions. You want to start a savings account for vacations and your partner argues that the house needs a new roof first. Let's meditate together in finding new ways to weave your dreams and necessities as one. Invite your partner or loved one to participate, if possible.

① Close your eyes and imagine a spiral stairway going upward. Each step represents a dream or a need that is important to both you and your loved one.

② As you secure a firm footing on each individual step, be mindful of the gradual ascent and subtle curvature of every step up. This is the woven path of every loving relationship.

③ Say aloud: "We are weaving our dreams and our needs together. Our staircase represents all of the various twists and turns that will lead us to where we need to be."

④ Take a silent moment to let this be so. ♡

94

---

dear mother and father

Poets say that we are evidence of the lives of our mothers and fathers, and their mothers and fathers, and theirs.

Becoming a parent, or observing a parent, can evoke understanding and gratitude for the sacrifices and blessings bestowed by parents.

Reflect upon your own mother and father with this practice:

① Take some protected time and find a place to breathe mind-fully for about a minute.

② Set your intention. For example: "May I remember my parents with kindness and be guided by wisdom."

③ Relax and rest deeply in mindful breathing.

④ Consciously recall either or both of your parents.

⑤ Remember a sacrifice they made for you. Let the ripples of that memory penetrate your heart.

⑥ Consider their gift of life, how your life flows from them. Acknowledge that.

⑦ Let thankfulness guide and support you. ♡

95

harmonize with reality

A half-glance at mainstream commercial media will reveal society's obsession with staying forever young. But you don't have to play into that beauty myth. Because no one can escape the natural aging process, prepare yourself to wholeheartedly embrace it with dignity, grace, and limitless splendor! To harmonize with reality means challenging yourself to learn how to be joyful, or at least carefree, about wrinkles, gray hair, a slowing gait, and declining strength.

① Take this moment to acknowledge the life force of ageless beauty that starts from within you and radiates outward through every smile, every act of kindness, and the breath of every generous spirit.

② Say aloud your affirmation several times: "I am a gorgeous, attractive, and magnificent being, inside and out, head to toe." Remember, you are not the sum of your aging body parts.

③ Assume the stature of royalty in this moment and be aware of your posture. Walk tall with pride for who you really are, and move with ease. ♡

96

it takes a village

Observing and reflecting on the lives of children—your own or others—quickly awakens one to the requirements of all human beings for love and guidance.

In any moment of a child's life, one can see an amazing web of support, intention, and interconnectedness operating.

Use this reflection on childhood to awaken a deeper love for all life:

① Breathe mindfully for about a minute.

② Set your intention. For example: "May this practice promote life."

③ Soften and open as much as feels safe to you while continuing to breathe mindfully.

④ Imagine yourself as a child. See the variety of requirements and conditions—people and things—that supported you. Recall supports for health, growth, protection, guidance, and sources of happiness and love.

⑤ Let each ripple of remembering fill and nourish you.

⑥ Let the recognition of interconnections guide you. ♡

97

memory game

Remember how you feel when you come across a sentimental gift from a loved one? Perhaps it's a ring you're wearing, a photograph, or a T-shirt from your last getaway. Take a trip down memory lane with a loved one, and share your stories.

① Try to recall an item or memory that captures that romantic feeling. If your loved one is present, share the story aloud. If you are alone, write it down to share later or call a friend and tell him about it.

② Think about why you selected that particular story. What emotions do you attach to it? What specific parts make it so sentimental and special? Was this something from long ago or just recently?

When you conjure your sweetly held memories, you infuse this moment with magic, love, and romance. Pocket this dreamy feeling in your heart. ♡

98

---

the way of not knowing

Ideas and data make up the way of knowing. Planning and predictability usually follow.

Do you also know the way of not knowing?

The way of not knowing embraces surprise, enjoys the unexpected, and welcomes wonder and mystery.

In the way of not knowing, you let go of the need to know or control, instead allowing life to come to you.

① Breathe mindfully for about a minute.

② Set your intention. For example: "May this practice help me live well."

③ Open your awareness to sounds and listen mindfully.

④ Allow all sounds and sensations. Be curious. What will happen next? Let it in.

⑤ Notice your thoughts. Hear them without fighting or feeding them. Appreciate their variety.

⑥ Relax. Let all your experiences come and go without resistance or control.

⑦ You do not have to know anything for this meditation. ♡

99

find the ocean in a seashell

As a child, you may have been told that you can hear the ocean inside a conch shell, if you really listen. There was something magical and wonderful and mysterious about this discovery. When your routine starts to get drab and mundane, discover the wonder hidden in secret places of your imagination.

①   Find an inanimate object to examine. It could be anything—a spool of thread, a chair, a tree.

②   Scan for parts of it that are simplistic as well as complex, ordinary as well as extraordinary. For example, your window is made of simple clear glass that's been cut into a square, but it is marvelous how the sunlight shines through, enveloping the room with its glimmering rays of warmth. Now you try it!

③   Do the same exercise with your relationship, noticing the components that are plain as well as the astonishing.

Stir up the extraordinary in every part of your life. This new outlook just might inspire you. ♡

entering the mystery

Love and life are filled with unknowns, and much is beyond our control.

Even the coming and going—the times and circumstances of birth and death, and the joys and sorrows in between—are mysterious and impossible to predict.

What wisdom might come if, even briefly, you opened more consciously to the truth of change and mortality?

①   Breathe mindfully for about a minute.

②   Set your intention. For example: "May this practice bring me peace."

③   Maintain steady attention on your breath—as steady as a mountain.

④   Open your heart and make some space—as much as feels safe.

⑤   Remember a loved one who has died. See how she was like you.

⑥   Recognize how all you love will leave you, or you will leave it. Have mercy and compassion for the fear of loss.

⑦   Let the preciousness of each life, and this moment, guide you. ♡

 Jeffrey Brantley, MD, is a consulting associate in the Duke Department of Psychiatry and the founder and director of the Mindfulness-Based Stress Reduction Program at Duke University's Center for Integrative Medicine. He has represented the Duke MBSR program in numerous radio, television, and print interviews. He is the best-selling author of *Calming Your Anxious Mind* and coauthor of *Five Good Minutes* and *Five Good Minutes in the Evening*.

Wendy Millstine, NC, is a freelance writer and certified holistic nutrition consultant who specializes in diet and stress reduction. She is coauthor of *Five Good Minutes* and *Five Good Minutes in the Evening*.

LP802   28